Chocolate everything

Cover Photo: Zuccotto, page 83

Opposite Photo:
Top: Marjolaine, page 86 (garnished with Fudge Icing, page 110, and chocolate filigrees, page 24)
Bottom: Chocolate Charlotte Russe, page 86 ("tied" with a pink ribbon)

Chocolate Everything
Copyright © Company's Coming Publishing Limited

All rights reserved worldwide. No part of this book may be reproduced, stored in a retrieval system or transmitted in any form by any means without written permission in advance from the publisher.

In the case of photocopying or other reprographic copying, a license may be purchased from the Canadian Copyright Licensing Agency (Access Copyright). Visit www.accesscopyright.ca or call toll free 1-800-893-5777. In the United States, please contact the Copyright Clearance Centre at www.copyright.com or call 978-646-8600.

Brief portions of this book may be reproduced for review purposes, provided credit is given to the source. Reviewers are invited to contact the publisher for additional information.

Fourth Printing February 2004

Canadian Cataloguing in Publication Data
Paré, Jean
Companys Coming, chocolate everything

(Special occasion series)
Includes index.
ISBN 1-895455-64-2

1. Cookery (Chocolate) I. Title. II. Title: Chocolate everything. III. Series: Paré, Jean, Special occasion series.

TX767.C5P35 2000 641.6'374 C00-900662-1

Published simultaneously in
Canada and the United States of America by
Company's Coming Publishing Limited
2311 – 96 Street
Edmonton, Alberta, Canada T6N 1G3
Tel: 780-450-6223 Fax: 780-450-1857
www.companyscoming.com

Company's Coming is a registered trademark owned by Company's Coming Publishing Limited

Color separations by
Friesens, Altona, Manitoba, Canada

Printed in China

Chocolate Everything was created thanks to the dedicated efforts of the people and organizations listed below.

COMPANY'S COMING PUBLISHING LIMITED

Author	Jean Paré
President	Grant Lovig
Vice President, Product Development	Kathy Knowles
Design Manager	Derrick Sorochan
Designer	Jaclyn Draker
Assistant Designer	Denise Hodgins
Typesetter	Marlene Crosbie

THE RECIPE FACTORY

Research & Development Manager	Nora Prokop
Copy Editors	Laurel Hoffmann
	Suzanne Hartman
Copywriter	Debbie Dixon
Proofreader	Mimi Tindall
Test Kitchen Supervisor	Lynda Elsenheimer
Test Kitchen Staff	Ellen Bunjevac
	Allison Dosman
	Jacquie Elton
	Linda Feniak
	Audrey Thomas
	Pat Yukes
Photographer	Stephe Tate Photo
Food Stylist	Carol MacLeod
Prop Stylist	Frieda Lovig
	Marcene Makovee
Nutrition Analyst	Margaret Ng, B.Sc., M.A., R.D.

Our special thanks to the following businesses for providing extensive props for photography.

The Bombay Company	Le Gnome
Chintz & Company	Salisbury Greenhouses & Landscaping
Clays Handmade Ceramic Tile & Stone	Stokes
Dansk Gifts	Stor-Age Revolution Inc.
Glasshouse	The Bay
La Cache	The Royal Doulton Store

Table of Contents

Foreword

I admit it! Chocolate is my favorite food! It's a true passion of mine—one of life's great pleasures that is shared by millions around the world. But it's here in North America, that more than half the total annual chocolate production is consumed (though not nearly enough in my home).

So, what is it that makes chocolate universally popular? Clearly it satisfies a natural craving for sweets, but so do many other foods. Or it may be that there are so many kinds of chocolate available to suit everyone's taste. What started out as a bitter drink enjoyed by the natives of the new world in the early 16th century has evolved to become a complex offering of dark, light, liquid, solid, bitter, sweet and semisweet chocolate.

Explore the intriguing history of chocolate and its evolution as a favorite, remarkable ingredient. The world of chocolate cuisine opens up with a spectacular selection of recipes to fulfill every sweet yearning.

Take our short course on the history of chocolate. Learn how a bitter ritual drink turned into frothy, rich hot chocolate. Impress others with your knowledge of the different types of chocolate and why white chocolate isn't really chocolate at all!

Dive into the section on decorating and garnishing. Be guided, step-by-step, through the process of making delicate and eye-catching filigrees, molds, curls and leaves. They are all so easy to make—and think of the compliments you'll receive.

Discover a mix of classic and contemporary recipes in chapters dedicated to beverages, cheesecakes, cakes, pies, desserts and squares. Exquisite color photographs will make you think you can eat right off the page! Don't be intimidated by our regal presentation—our garnishes and decorative touches are only suggestions. Imagination knows no limits!

If you are looking for some unique dinner ideas, try your hand at one of the main course recipes. This section features Mexican sauce or "mole" as it is known, which usually includes chili peppers, chocolate in some form and spices. Chili Mole and Spareribs Mole are two great examples of how chocolate can add a subtle flavor twist to any dish.

Our tour through the world of chocolate would not be complete without dedicating time and space to candies, fudges and cookies—well-loved decadent treats everyone looks forward to sampling. Not to be forgotten, is a comprehensive collection of recipes for chocolate icings, fillings and sauces—the finishing touch to any dessert. Take a moment to glance through our section on Special Touches and you will uncover a few more gems—easy to make Chocolate Cream Puffs, Chocolate Crêpes and Chocolate Cups. Even the divine Chocolate And Cherry Terrine can be assembled without difficulty when you follow the well-laid out "how-to" photos and instructions.

And what about the calories and cholesterol? Our first rule of thumb was to be mindful of the serving size—moderation is the key! Since it's difficult to adjust the fat grams found in chocolate, we have used lower-fat products for cream cheese, sour cream and whipped topping when suited to the recipe. In some recipes, we have indulged by using the real thing—whipping cream! Did you know that 1 cup (250 mL) of whipped cream contains 40.4 grams of fat, while 1 cup (250 mL) of frozen whipped topping is 15.6 grams, frozen light whipped topping is 9.6 grams and prepared dessert topping mix is only 6.8 grams? Regardless of which product you choose to use, they are, for the most part, interchangeable. We leave it to your discretion!

At first you might find it hard to imagine a book dedicated solely to chocolate. But aren't you glad it's true? The lowly cocoa bean, once revered in Central America as a food of the gods, has become a true obsession for millions of chocolate-lovers around the globe. It is my sincere hope that you will enjoy indulging in my passion for chocolate as much as I have enjoyed sharing it with you.

Jean Paré

The cocoa bean, or cacao bean to be more accurate, is found in tropical climates and resides inside a pod, with 20 to 40 other beans, on an evergreen cacao tree. It is harvested, roasted, crushed and eventually made into a thick chocolate liquor. This is where all chocolate begins and where the entire range of chocolate delicacies are born. This chapter offers you a brief history of chocolate and its evolution into the confection we recognize today.

Have you ever wondered if chocolate has gone bad when it turns white? Would you like to know the secret of chocolate-dipped cherries and molded candies? Learn how to melt, temper and mold chocolate; how to store it; and what to do when you have a problem with it. The answers are here and the recipes are waiting!

All about Chocolate

History of Chocolate

The history of chocolate is an amazing one, dating back over 3000 years to the Aztec and Maya Indians of Central America, most notably, Mexico. They enjoyed a drink called "xocolatl" or "chocolatl," meaning "bitter drink" or "bitter water," that was made from cocoa beans. This beverage was consumed at special occasions with the belief that the beans were a gift sown on earth by the gods and endowed wisdom if eaten. The beans themselves were also valued as a currency; slaves could be bought and sold for 100 cocoa beans!

Christopher Columbus learned of the cocoa bean during his explorations to this region of the Western Hemisphere. But it was the Spanish conquistador, Cortés, who brought "chocolatl" to Spain following the conquest of Mexico in 1519. As a drink, chocolate gained popularity fairly quickly once its bitter flavor was sweetened with sugar and vanilla. With that, hot chocolate was born!

The Spanish guarded their secret recipe for almost 100 years before the sweetened drink found its way into France and eventually all across Europe. An expensive luxury at the time, chocolate was first served in royal circles and later in fashionable and popular chocolate houses. Factories began to spring up during the 18th century in both Europe and North America. But chocolate remained an indulgence for only the rich until 1853 when its heavy import duties were dropped, sparking a burst of popularity among the general populace.

Chocolate was served only in liquid form for almost 300 years after its introduction to Europe, until a Dutch chemist found a way to separate the chocolate liquor into its two base ingredients, cocoa butter and cocoa powder. Within 25 years of his discovery, the first chocolate bar was manufactured.

Today, almost 500 years after Cortés sailed back to Spain with his precious cargo, you might say that chocolate has returned to its roots—some of the biggest chocolate producers in the world keep their home base on the shores of Central and North America. Indeed, the United States is one of the largest consumers of chocolate, cornering over 50% of the world market.

Cortés had no way of knowing the impact his discovery would have on the world. But for his foresight at recognizing the value in such a bitter and unappealing bean, chocolate-lovers everywhere thank him!

Zuccotto, page 83

Types of Chocolate

Bitter Chocolate - also called unsweetened, this is the darkest, purest form of chocolate liquor in its solid state; found in packages of six or eight 1 oz. (28 g) squares.

Semisweet Chocolate - solid form of chocolate that has had cocoa butter and sugar added but must contain at least 35% chocolate liquor.

Sweetened Chocolate - solid form of chocolate that has had even more sugar added than semisweet but must contain at least 15% chocolate liquor.

Milk Chocolate - lighter-colored sweetened chocolate; cocoa solids have been replaced with milk solids (or cream); more sensitive to overheating; best used in decorating and makes a nice color contrast on darker chocolate icing or glaze.

White Chocolate - not a true chocolate because it does not contain any chocolate liquor; but it does contain cocoa butter so it is sometimes referred to as a compound chocolate; also called confectioner's chocolate; because of the milk solids in white chocolate, it is more sensitive to heat than dark chocolate.

Chocolate Chips - designed and manufactured to hold their shape during the baking process; they cannot be used as a substitute for solid chocolate squares in baking; however, they can be melted in a saucepan and used in no-bake recipes such as mousses, sauces and icings.

Cocoa Powder - dried portion of chocolate nibs after the final amount of cocoa butter has been extracted; two types of powder: the milder Dutch-processed, which is alkalized, and the more bitter non-alkalized; both are the purest form of chocolate and contain no additives, preservatives and very little fat.

Chocolate Extract - a concentrated natural chocolate flavoring used to enhance chocolate flavor in recipes where regular chocolate is reduced to limit the fat grams.

Chocolate Talk

Bloom - gray film that forms on the outside of solid chocolate; occurs when stored at temperatures higher than 75°F (25°C); the cocoa butter begins to melt and rise to the surface; doesn't affect the flavor but has an unappetizing appearance; see Troubleshooting, page 11; see Tempering, page 12; see Storing, page 12.

Chocolate Liquor - thick, dark brown paste or liquor, "liquid essence," that results when chocolate nibs are ground to liquefy the cocoa butter; truly the essence of all chocolate.

Chocolate Nib - inner seed or "meat" of the cocoa bean; contains over 50% cocoa butter, making it very rich in flavor and calories!

Cocoa Bean - fruit from the cacao tree that is harvested for its inner chocolate nib, from which all chocolate evolves.

Cocoa Butter - vegetable fat that is found in chocolate nibs; its distinctive melting quality gives chocolate its unique texture.

Mexican Chocolate - solid chocolate flavored with cinnamon, almonds and vanilla.

Mole - from the Mexican word "molli" which means "concoction"; mole is a rich, dark brown sauce; main ingredient is chilies but can also include a small amount of Mexican (or bitter) chocolate.

Seize - term used when melted chocolate becomes lumpy and stiff; occurs when even just a drop of liquid comes in contact with it during heating, or when the chocolate is overheated; see Melting, page 12; see Troubleshooting, page 11.

Tempering - technique of stabilizing chocolate through a melting and cooling process; see Tempering, page 12.

Working with Chocolate

DO'S AND DON'TS

Chocolate is easy to work with, as long as you are aware of, and understand, a few basic facts:

1. Cut or break up chocolate into even-sized pieces for best control when melting.
2. Don't rush the melting process by turning up the heat under a double boiler. The higher heat will cause the water in the bottom pan to boil and create condensation on the bottom of the upper pan. This will, in turn, create too hot a temperature for the chocolate and it will burn.
3. Because chocolate will continue to melt after it has been removed from the heat source, only partially melt it, then remove and continue stirring until completely melted and smooth. This works especially well if melting larger quantities (over 8 oz., 225 g) of chocolate.
4. Never cover the saucepan or bowl while melting chocolate—even the smallest drop of condensation will cause the chocolate to seize; see Chocolate Talk, page 10; see Troubleshooting, below.
5. Milk chocolate and white chocolate will burn and seize more quickly and easily than darker semisweet chocolate, so watch them carefully.
6. Always have the rest of the ingredients at room temperature before starting a recipe containing chocolate.

TROUBLESHOOTING

1. Can chocolate that has seized be restored to its smooth texture? Yes. Add 1 tsp. (5 mL) cooking oil or solid shortening (not butter or margarine) per 1 oz. (28 g) chocolate and stir. Repeat until chocolate has regained its smoothness.
2. Can burned chocolate be saved? No, once the taste has been altered it can't be rescued.
3. When should chocolate be chilled and when should it be stored at room temperature? Anything made with tempered chocolate should be stored at room temperature. If untempered chocolate has been used, place the finished product in the refrigerator immediately to harden the fat crystals and maintain the glossy finish.
4. When baking with chocolate I find it makes a mess of my dishcloth and apron. How do I remove the stains? Presoak the items with a commercial presoak, or spray with a laundry stain remover. If the item can be bleached, do so only after presoaking.
5. Can I use tub margarine when a recipe calls for butter or margarine? Do not use the soft tub margarines (regular or low-fat) or other low-fat spreads in baking as they contain a higher percentage of water and will react differently when heated, causing unsatisfactory results.
6. Substitutions:

a) one 1 oz. (28 g) unsweetened chocolate square
= 3 tbsp. (50 mL) cocoa + 1 tbsp. (15 mL) shortening, hard margarine or butter

b) six 1 oz. (28 g) semisweet chocolate squares
= 1 cup (250 mL) semisweet chocolate chips
= 6 tbsp. (100 mL) cocoa + 7 tbsp. (115 mL) granulated sugar + 1/4 cup (60 mL) shortening, hard margarine or butter
= two 1 oz. (28 g) unsweetened chocolate squares + 7 tbsp. (115 mL) granulated sugar + 2 tbsp. (30 mL) shortening, hard margarine or butter

c) four 1 oz. (28 g) sweetened chocolate squares (total of 4 oz., 113 g)
= 1/4 cup (60 mL) cocoa + 1/3 cup (75 mL) granulated sugar + 3 tbsp. (50 mL) shortening, hard margarine or butter

Melting

Melting chocolate is a simple but sensitive process. Excessive heat will scorch chocolate and even the slightest drop of moisture will cause melting chocolate to become lumpy. Chocolate can simply be melted for use in general baking, (cakes, icings, cookies and some desserts) or tempered, see below, for decorative uses such as glazes, molds and decorations.

A cool room, 65 to 70°F (18 to 21°C) is the best place to work with chocolate. The chocolate will set quickly with no need for refrigeration. If the room temperature is higher, chill the chocolate to set.

Melting Instructions–Stovetop

1. Place chocolate (broken into even-sized pieces) either in double boiler over hot (never boiling) water that doesn't touch bottom of upper pan, in glass measuring cup or bowl set in larger pan of very hot tap water, or in heavy saucepan on lowest heat.
2. Constantly stir chocolate just until smooth. Remove from heat immediately. (See Do's And Don'ts, page 11, for melting larger quantities).

Melting Instructions–Microwave

1. Place chocolate in microwave-safe plastic bowl. Microwave, uncovered, on medium (50%) for up to 3 minutes, stirring gently after each minute, until smooth.
2. Heat in microwave in increasingly shorter time increments until most of chocolate is melted. Place bowl on work surface and stir until all chocolate is smooth and shiny.

Tempering

Tempering is achieved by heating and cooling chocolate to a specific temperature, causing one of its main ingredients, cocoa butter, to form crystals. This ensures that the chocolate coating will stay firm and glossy without refrigeration or the addition of wax. And the good news is—it doesn't have to be the highest (and most expensive) quality of chocolate. But don't use chocolate chips, as they are formulated to hold their shape in baking.

It is best to melt about 8 oz. (225 g) chocolate at any one time. This amount gives you enough depth in the saucepan to be able to get an accurate temperature reading. Any left over can be cooled, stored and remelted.

Once chocolate has been tempered, it needs only to be melted to be used.

Tempering Instructions

1. Melt about ⅔ of needed amount of chocolate in small bowl set in pan of hot (not boiling) water. Water level must be well below rim of bowl to avoid getting liquid in chocolate.
2. Heat chocolate to 115°F (45°C) for dark chocolate and 110°F (43°C) for white and milk chocolate, stirring frequently with rubber spatula and scraping down sides and bottom of bowl, so that chocolate is evenly and uniformly heated. Be sure to use candy thermometer.
3. When chocolate reaches correct temperature, remove bowl from water. Immediately add remaining ⅓ of unmelted chocolate. Continue stirring and scraping until all chocolate has melted and cooled to less than 90°F (32°C).

Storing

Tempered chocolate, wrapped tightly or placed in an airtight container, will stay fresh for at least a year in a cool, dry place, preferably below 75°F (25°C) and above 65°F (18°C).

Don't store chocolate in the refrigerator unless the room temperature is above 75°F (25°C). If you do keep chocolate in the refrigerator or freezer for any length of time, wrap it tightly. Any moisture that seeps inside the package is likely to change the chocolate's texture.

Milk and white chocolate should not be stored for longer than about 9 months due to the milk solids they contain.

Chocolate-Covered Pretzels

An attractive addition to a plate of sweets. Makes a pretty gift and so easy to do! Drizzle with contrasting color of chocolate for special effect.

White chocolate dipping wafers	**½ cup**	**125 mL**
Dark chocolate dipping wafers	**½ cup**	**125 mL**
Mini pretzels		

Heat both chocolates separately in small saucepan over hot water, or on low, stirring constantly, until melted. Do not overheat. Remove from heat.

Drop 16 pretzels, 1 at a time, into dark chocolate to coat. Lift out with fork. Allow to drip back into saucepan. Place coated pretzels on waxed paper. Repeat with remaining 16 pretzels in white chocolate. Makes 16 dark and 16 white covered pretzels.

1 coated pretzel: 35 Calories; 1 g Protein; 2 g Total Fat; 4 g Carbohydrate; 36 mg Sodium; trace Dietary Fiber

Pictured on this page.

Dipped Strawberries

Coating is thin, rich, dark and shiny. Be creative and use both dark and white chocolate.

Semisweet chocolate baking squares (1 oz., 28 g, each), cut up	**3**	**3**
Grated paraffin wax	**1 tbsp.**	**15 mL**
Small, nicely shaped strawberries, with stems	**30**	**30**

Melt chocolate and paraffin wax in small saucepan over hot water, or on low, stirring constantly, until smooth. Do not overheat. Pour into custard cup.

Holding strawberry by stem end, dip straight down into chocolate ¾ way up strawberry. Set, stem end down, on waxed paper. Makes 30.

1 dipped strawberry: 17 Calories; trace Protein; 1 g Total Fat; 2 g Carbohydrate; trace Sodium; trace Dietary Fiber

Pictured on this page.

Top: Chocolate-Covered Pretzels
Bottom: Dipped Strawberries

Chocolate Cherries

Fabulous! Have fun making your own. Will keep for up to 8 weeks at room temperature. Chill if keeping longer.

Maraschino cherries, with stems	**60**	**60**
Fondant:		
Marshmallow crème	**⅔ cup**	**150 mL**
Hard margarine, softened	**2 tbsp.**	**30 mL**
Almond flavoring	**½ tsp.**	**2 mL**
Icing (confectioner's) sugar	**1⅓ cups**	**325 mL**
Coating:		
Dark tempered chocolate, page 12	**1 lb.**	**454 g**

Spread cherries on paper towel. Drain overnight.

Fondant: Beat marshmallow crème, margarine and almond flavoring in medium bowl until smooth. Gradually beat in icing sugar. Turn out onto counter. If too sticky, work in a bit more icing sugar. Flatten 1 tsp., 5 mL, (or marble-size piece) fondant, then mold and place around cherry, covering completely.

Coating: Melt chocolate in small saucepan over hot water, or on low, stirring constantly, until smooth. Do not overheat. Pour some of melted chocolate into small narrow glass. Place glass in bowl of warm water. Holding cherry by stem, dip into chocolate to completely coat. Allow excess to drip back into glass. Place on waxed paper. Let set. Redip bottoms, if necessary to seal completely. Let stand at room temperature for at least 2 days for fondant layer to liquefy. Makes about 5 dozen.

1 covered cherry: 63 Calories; 1 g Protein; 3.4 g Total Fat; 10 g Carbohydrate; 6 mg Sodium; trace Dietary Fiber

Pictured on page 15.

Fruit And Nut Clusters

Add dried fruit and nuts to leftover chocolate. Drop by spoonfuls onto waxed paper.

Chocolate Cherries, above

Molding Chocolate

Chocolate is actually very easy to shape and mold into creative and unique designs. Craft stores that carry chocolate-making supplies can have a wide variety of preshaped molds for candies. Or, using the basic directions below for making our chocolate box, create your own box, basket or container to hold your homemade chocolates or other treats.

Remember that a cooler room or at least a cool working surface will make working with chocolate much easier. Watch your fingers too—you will leave visible fingerprints if your hands are warm!

Candy Molds

Using remelted tempered chocolate, page 12, fill desired molds. When filled, gently tap mold on counter to smooth out chocolate and release any air bubbles. Place mold in refrigerator or freezer for two or three minutes, then flip out onto waxed paper. Have two molds of your favorite shapes to speed up the process.

Chocolate Box

You can make this box any size you like.

Chocolate dipping wafers (or pure dark tempered chocolate, page 12)	**8 oz.**	**225 g**

Tape down 17 x 18 inch (42.5 x 45 cm) waxed (or parchment) paper rectangle on flat surface. Melt chocolate. Spread evenly with long spreader to 1/8 inch (3 mm) thickness. Chill.

1. Lay clean ruler on chocolate. Use sharp knife to cut straight edges to match the following dimensions: one 4 x 4 inch (10 x 10 cm) base, four 3 7/8 x 2 inch (9.7 x 5 cm) sides.

2. Lift base onto clean piece of waxed paper or parchment paper. "Glue" sides, 1 at a time, using remelted chocolate and paintbrush. Chill. A lid can be made using same method as above. Drizzle melted white chocolate over lid and sides for added decoration.

Pictured on page 17.

Chocolate Box, page 16, with Molded Chocolates, page 16

Decorating with chocolate

It's time to have some fun! Try your hand at creating a delicate filigree, or learn simple tricks for making flawless chocolate curls. Gourmet chefs know full well the value of using dramatic chocolate garnishes. Decorating with chocolate is actually quite simple with just a little practice and patience. This section comes complete with step-by-step pictured instructions that anyone—novice or expert—can follow for perfect results. Chocolate has the wonderful ability to be melted, molded or sculpted without any change to its rich flavor. That means you are free to fully explore your artistic talents.

Cake Decorating

We often ooh and aah when we see a special cake covered with icing that dips, swirls and squiggles. Having the right tools (and a steady hand) are all you need to create the icing designs you see throughout this book.

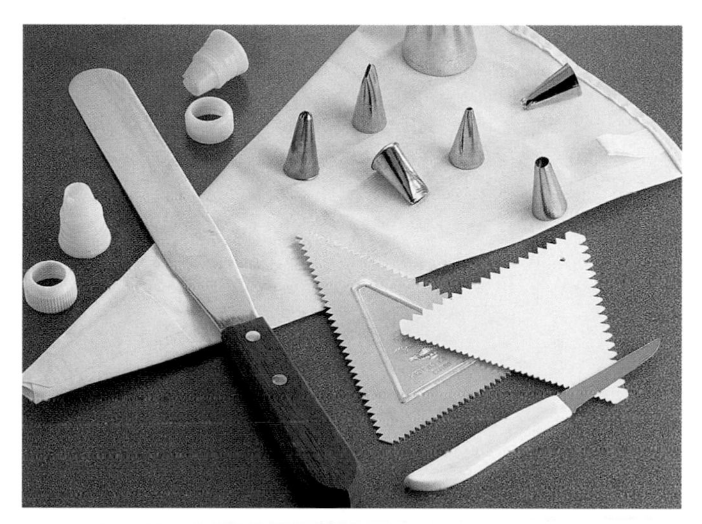

1. Piping bag or pastry bag, and choice of 6 or 7 tips or nozzles (see Tip samples), below; tools that create decorative lines in icing; proper spreading knife.

2. Starting from top: Large Tip (#1B)
   Star Tip (#21)
   Rose Tip (#104)
   Specialty Tip (#96)
   Open Star Tip (#172)

Grated/Shaved Chocolate

Grated or shaved chocolate is perfect for a quick and easy garnish. Use a larger piece of hardened tempered chocolate, page 12, for easy handling. If your hands are very warm, hold the chocolate in a piece of waxed paper to prevent melting. Use a spoon to sprinkle chocolate after grating or shaving since it melts very quickly in your fingers. Store in a covered container in the refrigerator indefinitely.

GRATED

Chill chocolate before beginning so that it is firm. Working against grater, hold both grater and chocolate firmly, letting chocolate shreds fall onto piece of waxed paper. Use different sizes on grater to achieve different looks.

SHAVED

Have chocolate at room temperature so that it will curl slightly. Scrape chocolate firmly along its length with sharp, swivel-type vegetable peeler. For narrower shavings, use flat underside of peeler.

Cutouts, Curls, and Caraque

To make cutouts, curls and caraque (cah-RACK), pour remelted tempered chocolate, page 12, onto clean, smooth surface such as marble slab or large cookie or baking sheet, turned upside down. Spread chocolate across surface with even strokes with spatula to about 1/16 inch (1.5 mm) thickness. Chocolate should be even thickness without deep ridges.

Let chocolate set at room temperature until firm. For rounded edges, place plastic wrap over chocolate before cutting out shapes. Place cookie cutter on plastic wrap. Press firmly. Lift cookie cutter straight off. Repeat until entire surface has been used. Remove plastic wrap carefully. Lift shapes off with metal spatula.

Let chocolate set at room temperature until firm. Using scraper, start 1 inch (2.5 cm) from nearest edge of chocolate. Push scraper away from you at 25° angle across surface of chocolate until large curl forms. Use wooden pick to lift each curl off board, as it is made, to chilled plate or container. Or place directly on cake.

Let chocolate set at room temperature until firm. Brace board against body. Starting about 2 inches (5 cm) from far left corner of board, pull large-bladed knife towards you at 45° angle, scraping along chocolate to form long curl that is pointed at one end.

Use wooden pick to lift each piece of caraque off board, as it is made, to chilled plate or container. Or place directly on cake.

Leaves

Use pliable leaves with well-defined veins, such as mint, lemon or salal, available at most florist shops. Be sure leaves are cleaned and dry.

1. Remelt small amount of tempered chocolate, page 12, in saucepan on low. Hold leaf, underside up, in one hand. Using small brush, coat layer of chocolate on leaf. Place, coated side up, on waxed paper on plate. Chill until set.

2. Carefully peel leaf away from chocolate.

3. For variegated look, smear white chocolate over part of leaf with finger. Brush dark chocolate over all. Proceed as in steps 1 and 2.

Drizzling

Drizzling is one of those really easy decorating techniques that turns a plain-looking dessert into a showpiece. For easy handling and best results, fill piping bag, or unpleated freezer bag, only half full with melted chocolate.

DRIZZLING–RANDOM PATTERN

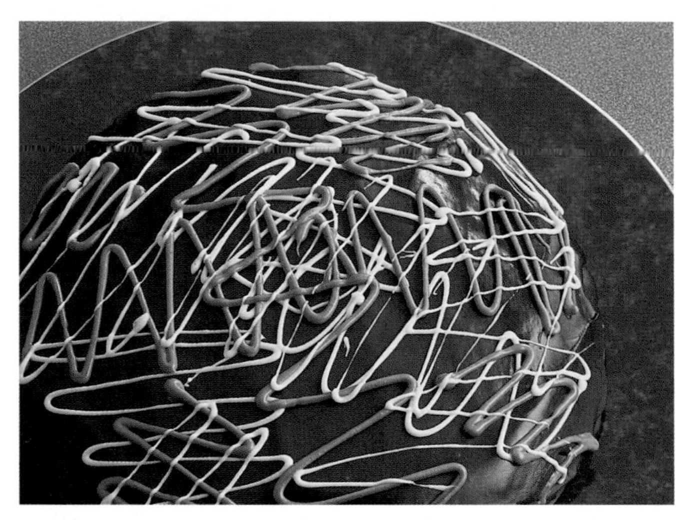

Pipe chocolate (white, dark or combination) onto cake using random zigzag motion.

DRIZZLING–SPIDER WEB PATTERN

Pipe chocolate in concentric circles on top of icing. Starting at center, draw tip of knife or wooden pick through lines to outer edge. Continue around cake at even intervals. You can also start at edge and draw toward center. Whichever direction is preferred, don't change once you start!

DRIZZLING–FEATHERED PATTERN

Pipe chocolate in parallel lines (or concentric circles) over icing. Draw thin knife or wooden pick from edge to edge (or to center) through lines. Continue, alternating direction of every other line, and keeping lines parallel.

DRIZZLING–HEART PATTERN

Pipe drops of sauce or chocolate onto icing at even intervals. Draw thin knife or wooden pick through middle of circles, starting at top circle and not stopping until final heart has been formed.

Tip: To help you keep your chocolate lines parallel, first lightly mark the top of the cake using a knife and a ruler or template. Pipe the chocolate following the markings.

Marbling

1. Pour main amount of liquid, batter or chocolate into appropriate baking dish or pan. Spoon dabs of contrasting ingredient over top.

2. Cut zigzag, swirling pattern through batter. Do not overmix or marbling effect will be lost.

Glazing

Place cake on rack on top of parchment or waxed paper on working surface. Pour glaze onto top of cake at center, allowing glaze to drip down sides. Spread quickly with spatula or spreader to fully cover cake.

Cocoa Glaze

Makes a dark, shiny glaze.

Cocoa, sifted	**¼ cup**	**60 mL**
Corn syrup	**2 tbsp.**	**30 mL**
Hard margarine	**2 tbsp.**	**30 mL**
Milk	**¼ cup**	**60 mL**
Vanilla	**¼ tsp.**	**1 mL**
Icing (confectioner's) sugar	**2 cups**	**500 mL**

Stir first 5 ingredients in medium saucepan on low until margarine is melted. Remove from heat.

Beat in icing sugar, adding more milk or icing sugar as needed to make barely pourable consistency. Makes 1¼ cups (300 mL).

2 tbsp. (30 mL): 129 Calories; 1 g Protein; 2.5 g Total Fat; 28 g Carbohydrate; 32 mg Sodium; 1 g Dietary Fiber

Pictured on page 105.

Chocolate Glaze

Smooth and rich. Easy to double.

Whipping cream (or evaporated milk)	**¾ cup**	**175 mL**
Semisweet chocolate baking squares (1 oz., 28 g, each), cut up	**6**	**6**

Heat whipping cream in small saucepan on low. Add chocolate, stirring constantly, until melted and smooth. Makes about 1 cup (250 mL).

1 tbsp. (15 mL): 90 Calories; 1 g Protein; 7.5 g Total Fat; 6 g Carbohydrate; 6 mg Sodium; 1 g Dietary Fiber

Pictured on front cover, page 9 and page 84/85.

Filigrees

Filigrees are those hard chocolate squiggles found on top of fancy desserts. They make a dish of chocolate mousse or a plain piece of cheesecake much more special. Keep filigrees chilled as they will soften quickly from the warmth of your hand. When choosing your designs, keep in mind that although these are simple to make, they are fragile if too long or too thin. If you have a longer or more open design, try creating ways to "connect" the lines for added strength.

TO MAKE FILIGREES

Draw desired shape(s) on piece of plain white paper or use page that you wish to trace. Place piece of waxed paper over drawings or page and tape in place. Use tempered chocolate, page 12, that has been remelted; allow to cool slightly. Pour melted chocolate into piping (or pastry) bag fitted with smallest tip, or into non-pleated freezer bag. If using freezer bag, snip very tiny hole across one corner. Pipe chocolate evenly, tracing over designs. Let stand until dry and hard. Carefully lift chocolate design off waxed paper with thin metal spatula.

FILIGREES–SAMPLES

Beside and below are samples of the many different designs that you can make. White and dark chocolate can be mixed for great contrasts. Words or letters can be traced to personalize individual servings or to mark special occasions.

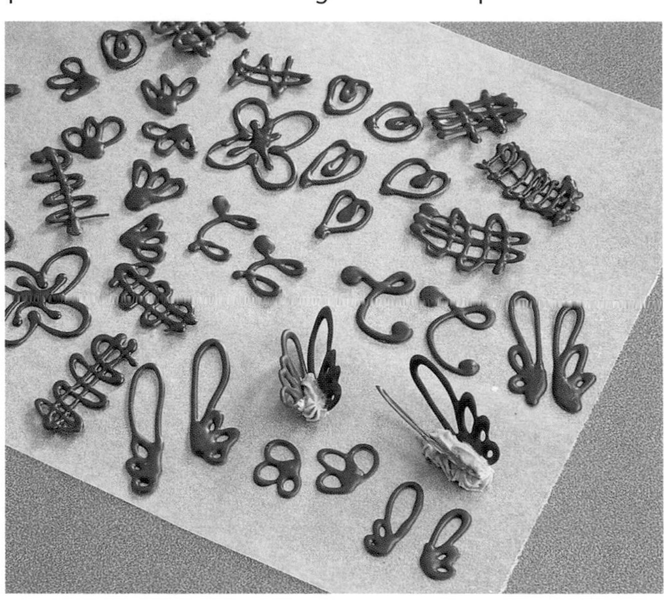

FILIGREES–CURVED

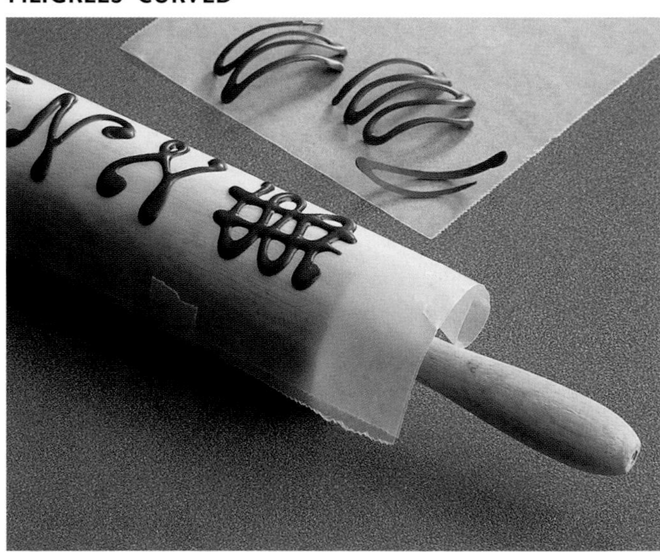

Tape waxed paper on rolling pin. Pipe desired design evenly over top portion of curve of rolling pin. Let set. Gently lift paper from rolling pin. Carefully peel paper from chocolate design.

Hot chocolate was the first known chocolate beverage to become popular, but it wasn't the first one to be made with cocoa. The earliest chocolate drink was an unappealing bitter brew of cocoa and chilies consumed by the Aztec and Maya Indians more than three thousand years ago. It wasn't until the Europeans added sugar, vanilla and a little heat in the sixteenth century that Hot Chocolate became the royal beverage of choice. Of course, like every great recipe, this timeless classic has become the inspiration for an endless number of other chocolate beverages. In this chapter, you'll find an exotic sampling of recipes such as Mocha Punch and Special Mint Drink. You may even wish to forego dessert in favor of one of these delectable and very relaxing drinks.

Beverages

Mocha Punch

Chocolate syrup in the bottom of each glass gives this a very different look. Serve the syrup in a small pitcher on one side of the punch bowl and have a bucket of ice on the other side. Whipped topping and Grated Chocolate, page 19, finish this off.

Cold strong coffee	**4 cups**	**1 L**
Granulated sugar	**1/2 cup**	**125 mL**
Salt	**1/4 tsp.**	**1 mL**
Cold strong coffee	**4 cups**	**1 L**
Chocolate ice cream	**4 cups**	**1 L**
Vanilla ice cream	**4 cups**	**1 L**
Almond flavoring	**1/4 tsp.**	**1 mL**
Chocolate Syrup, page 174	**3/4 cup**	**175 mL**
Ice cubes	**36**	**36**

Stir first amount of coffee, sugar and salt in punch bowl until sugar dissolves.

Add next 4 ingredients. Stir to melt ice cream. Makes about 11 cups (2.75 L) coffee mixture.

Measure 1 tbsp. (15 mL) syrup into bottom of each glass. Add 3 ice cubes. Fill with punch. Do not stir. Makes 11 servings.

1 serving: 274 Calories; 4 g Protein; 11.1 g Total Fat; 41 g Carbohydrate; 165 mg Sodium; 1 g Dietary Fiber

Pictured on this page.

White Chocolate Shake

Thick, creamy and frothy. A stemmed maraschino cherry nestled on top is a pretty color contrast with this very white drink.

Milk	1 cup	250 mL
White Chocolate Ice Cream, page 100	2 cups	500 mL
White corn syrup	2 tsp.	10 mL
Instant vanilla pudding powder	1 tbsp.	15 mL

Process all 4 ingredients in blender. Pour into 2 glasses. Makes 2⅔ cups (650 mL). Serves 2.

1 serving: 675 Calories; 12 g Protein; 39.1 g Total Fat; 70 g Carbohydrate; 463 mg Sodium; trace Dietary Fiber

Pictured on page 29.

Peanut Chocolate Shake

This is so good and so simple. No extra garnish required.

Rounded scoops of vanilla or chocolate ice cream	2	2
Milk	½ cup	125 mL
Smooth peanut butter	1½ tbsp.	25 mL
Chocolate Syrup, page 174	1 tbsp.	15 mL

Combine all 4 ingredients in blender. Process until smooth. Makes 1⅓ cups (325 mL). Serves 1.

1 serving: 544 Calories; 16 g Protein; 30.4 g Total Fat; 57 g Carbohydrate; 326 mg Sodium; 2 g Dietary Fiber

Pictured on page 29.

Coffee Alexander Shake

A variation of a favorite cocktail. Whipped topping and Chocolate Curls, page 20, are a quick finishing touch.

Boiling water	¼ cup	60 mL
Instant coffee granules	2 tsp.	10 mL
Milk	1 cup	250 mL
Chocolate Syrup, page 174	2 tbsp.	30 mL
Vanilla ice cream	1 cup	250 mL

Stir boiling water and coffee granules in small cup. Cool.

Put milk, syrup, ice cream and prepared coffee into blender. Process until smooth. Pour into 2 fancy stemware glasses. Makes 2 cups (500 mL). Serves 2.

1 serving: 225 Calories; 7 g Protein; 9 g Total Fat; 30 g Carbohydrate; 140 mg Sodium; 1 g Dietary Fiber

Pictured on page 29.

Chocolate Orange Shake

Refreshing. Not too sweet—unless you add a final garnish of whipped topping!

Prepared orange juice	1⅓ cups	325 mL
Ginger ale	1 cup	250 mL
Rounded scoops of chocolate ice cream	3	3

Pour orange juice and ginger ale into blender. Add ice cream. Process until smooth. Makes 2½ cups (625 mL). Serves 2.

1 serving: 334 Calories; 5 g Protein; 11.5 g Total Fat; 55 g Carbohydrate; 103 mg Sodium; 1 g Dietary Fiber

Pictured on page 29.

Top: Chocolate Orange Shake, this page
Center Left: Coffee Alexander Shake, this page
Center Right: White Chocolate Shake, this page
Bottom: Peanut Chocolate Shake, this page

Chocolate Coffee

Both chocolate and coffee flavors are noticeable. Try this with a dollop of whipped topping embedded with a Chocolate Filigree, page 24.

Milk	**1 cup**	**250 mL**
Instant chocolate drink powder	**1 tbsp.**	**15 mL**
Instant coffee granules	**2 tsp.**	**10 mL**
Salt, a very tiny pinch (optional)		

Heat milk in mug on high (100%) in microwave until almost boiling, about 2 minutes.

Stir in drink powder, coffee granules and salt if using. Serves 1.

1 serving: 155 Calories; 9 g Protein; 3.1 g Total Fat; 24 g Carbohydrate; 153 mg Sodium; 0 g Dietary Fiber

Pictured on page 31.

Mocha Café

Excellent in taste and appearance. Enhance both with a garnish of whipped topping and Grated Chocolate, page 19.

Strong coffee	**½ cup**	**125 mL**
Milk	**½ cup**	**125 mL**
Instant chocolate drink powder	**1 tbsp.**	**15 mL**

Stir coffee, milk and drink powder in glass mug. Microwave on high (100%) for 2 minutes or until very hot. Serves 1.

1 serving: 97 Calories; 5 g Protein; 1.7 g Total Fat; 17 g Carbohydrate; 92 mg Sodium; 0 g Dietary Fiber

Pictured on page 31.

1. Café Vienna, page 32
2. Mocha Café, this page
3. Special Mint Drink, page 32
4. Chocolate Coffee, this page

Café Vienna

A good rainy day or chilly evening drink. For added flair, brush rims of empty glasses with Crème de Cacao liqueur, then dip into sugar.

Milk	**1 cup**	**250 mL**
Instant coffee granules	**1½ tsp.**	**7 mL**
Ground cinnamon, just a pinch		
Crème de Cacao liqueur	**2 tbsp.**	**30 mL**

Heat milk, coffee granules and cinnamon in small saucepan until steaming hot.

Stir in liqueur. Pour into mug. Makes 1 cup (250 mL). Serves 1.

1 serving: 218 Calories; 10 g Protein; 7.7 g Total Fat; 20 g Carbohydrate; 159 mg Sodium; 0 g Dietary Fiber

Pictured on page 30/31.

Creamy Mocha

It doesn't get any easier than this. Garnish with whipped topping and a chocolate-covered coffee bean.

Milk	**1 cup**	**250 mL**
Instant chocolate drink powder	**2 tbsp.**	**30 mL**
Instant coffee granules	**1½ tsp.**	**7 mL**
Powdered coffee whitener	**1 tsp.**	**5 mL**

Heat milk in large mug in microwave on high (100%) for about 2 minutes until almost boiling.

Add drink powder, coffee granules and coffee whitener. Whisk to dissolve. Sprinkle with chocolate. Makes 1 serving.

1 serving: 220 Calories; 10 g Protein; 5.2 g Total Fat; 36 g Carbohydrate; 181 mg Sodium; 0 g Dietary Fiber

Pictured on page 33.

Special Mint Drink

Good served hot or cold. Add a drop of green food coloring to whipped topping garnish to give a hint of the mint flavor to come. Add a chocolate filligree if desired.

Cocoa, sifted	**3 tbsp.**	**50 mL**
Granulated sugar	**⅓ cup**	**75 mL**
Milk	**¼ cup**	**60 mL**
Milk	**5½ cups**	**1.4 L**
Crème de Cacao liqueur	**3 tbsp.**	**50 mL**
White Crème de Menthe liqueur	**3 tbsp.**	**50 mL**

Mix cocoa, sugar and first amount of milk in large saucepan. Heat on medium-low, stirring constantly, until cocoa and sugar are dissolved.

Add second amount of milk. Stir. Add both liqueurs. Stir to heat through. Pour into 6 mugs. Makes about 6 cups (1.5 L). Serves 6.

1 serving: 211 Calories; 9 g Protein; 4.1 g Total Fat; 30 g Carbohydrate; 131 mg Sodium; 1 g Dietary Fiber

Pictured on page 31.

White Hot Chocolate

Serve this—most likely no one will know what it is. Keep the steam in with a mound of whipped topping, a sprinkle of Shaved Chocolate, page 19, and a cinnamon stick.

Milk	**4 cups**	**1 L**
White chocolate baking squares (1 oz., 28 g, each), cut up	**4**	**4**
Almond flavoring	**¼ tsp.**	**1 mL**

Heat milk in large saucepan until scalding hot.

Stir in chocolate until melted. Add almond flavoring. Stir. Pour into 4 mugs. Serves 4.

1 serving: 269 Calories; 10 g Protein; 11.7 g Total Fat; 29 g Carbohydrate; 154 mg Sodium; 0 g Dietary Fiber

Pictured on page 33.

Top: Creamy Mocha, this page
Bottom: White Hot Chocolate, this page

Chocolate Soda

Or a chocolate float. Notice the color changes as you pour soda water over the dark base.

Chocolate milk (see Note)	**½ cup**	**125 mL**
Rounded scoop of vanilla or chocolate ice cream	**1**	**1**
Soda water	**1 cup**	**250 mL**

Pour chocolate milk into 16 oz. (500 mL) glass. Add ice cream. Pour soda water slowly into glass until full. Serve with straw and long soda spoon. Makes 2 cups (500 mL). Serves 1.

1 serving: 237 Calories; 7 g Protein; 10.2 g Total Fat; 30 g Carbohydrate; 168 mg Sodium; 1 g Dietary Fiber

Pictured on page 35.

Note: 1½ tbsp. (25 mL) instant chocolate drink powder or 1 tbsp. (15 mL) chocolate syrup stirred into ½ cup (125 mL) milk may be used instead of chocolate milk.

Malted Milk Shake

Nice malt flavor. This is so frothy—makes a great mustache!

Milk	**1 cup**	**250 mL**
Chocolate ice cream	**2 cups**	**500 mL**
Chocolate syrup	**2 tbsp.**	**30 mL**
Malted milk drink powder (such as Ovaltine)	**2 tbsp.**	**30 mL**

Combine all 4 ingredients in blender. Process until thick and smooth. Makes 3 cups (750 mL). Serves 3.

1 serving: 284 Calories; 7 g Protein; 11.5 g Total Fat; 40 g Carbohydrate; 160 mg Sodium; trace Dietary Fiber

Pictured on page 35.

Malted Banana Shake

Add 1 banana, cut up, to blender. Pleasant refreshing taste.

Chocolate Orange Drink

Refreshing drink. The orange flavor dominates.

Prepared orange juice	**1 cup**	**250 mL**
Cocoa, sifted	**1 tbsp.**	**15 mL**
Granulated sugar	**1 tbsp.**	**15 mL**
Vanilla	**⅛ tsp.**	**0.5 mL**
Crushed ice	**½ cup**	**125 mL**

Combine all 5 ingredients in blender. Process until smooth. Pour over crushed ice. Makes 1⅔ cups (400 mL). Serves 1.

1 serving: 178 Calories; 3 g Protein; 0.6 g Total Fat; 44 g Carbohydrate; 3 mg Sodium; 4 g Dietary Fiber

Pictured on page 35.

Chocolate Syrup Drink

Omit cocoa and sugar. Add 2 to 3 tbsp. (30 to 50 mL) chocolate syrup.

Left: Chocolate Soda, this page
Center: Chocolate Orange Drink, above
Right: Malted Milk Shake, this page

Chocolate lovers will tell you that all cakes are not created equal! In fact, it would be their pleasure to gladly argue the finer points of a chocolate cake versus any other cake to anyone willing to listen. A welcome feature of these recipes is not only that they are chocolate, but that they offer you a choice between making a rich and sweet or more subtly flavored cake. Chocoholics will adore Chocolate Pound Cake while others will appreciate the delicate taste of a Pumpkin Chip Cake. And, of course, what could be more memorable than a classic chocolate cake, except maybe when it's also fat-free? If you think you need a special occasion, then celebrate the beauty of a sunset or the smile of a child with one of these delicious cakes.

Black Forest Decadence

A real showpiece. Chocolate layers filled with cherry-cream and topped with a chocolate glaze. Crown with stemmed maraschino cherries.

Dark chocolate cake mix (2 layer size)	**1**	**1**
Whipping cream (or 4 cups, 1 L, whipped topping)	**2 cups**	**500 mL**
Icing (confectioner's) sugar	**1 tbsp.**	**15 mL**
Can of cherry pie filling	**19 oz.**	**540 mL**
Glaze:		
Semisweet chocolate baking squares (1 oz., 28 g, each), cut up	**6**	**6**
Light cream (half-and-half)	**½ cup**	**125 mL**

Prepare cake according to package directions. Bake in 2 greased 9 inch (22 cm) round layer pans. Cool. Turn out onto rack. Split each to make 4 layers.

Beat whipping cream and icing sugar in large bowl until stiff. Reserve 1 cup (250 mL) for garnish.

Fold pie filling into remaining whipped cream. Spread ⅓ cherry-cream mixture over 3 layers, stacking as each is spread. Add fourth layer to top.

Glaze: Melt chocolate with light cream in medium saucepan on low, stirring constantly, until smooth. Set pan in cold water. Whisk until cooled enough to be slightly pourable. Drizzle over top of cake, allowing some to run down sides. Chill. Garnish with reserved whipped cream. Cuts into 16 wedges.

1 wedge: 430 Calories; 3 g Protein; 28.3 g Total Fat; 45 g Carbohydrate; 205 mg Sodium; 1 g Dietary Fiber

Pictured on this page.

Pumpkin Chip Cake

This is moist with a pumpkin flavor. Almost the texture of a pound cake.

Large eggs	4	4
Granulated sugar	2 cups	500 mL
Can of pumpkin (without spices)	14 oz.	398 mL
Cooking oil	3/4 cup	175 mL
All-purpose flour	2 cups	500 mL
Baking powder	2 tsp.	10 mL
Baking soda	1 tsp.	5 mL
Ground cinnamon	2 tsp.	10 mL
Salt	3/4 tsp.	4 mL
Cocoa, sifted	1/4 cup	60 mL
Semisweet chocolate chips	1 cup	250 mL
Chocolate Whipped Topping, page 109		

Beat eggs until frothy. Beat in sugar. Add pumpkin and cooking oil. Beat.

Stir next 6 ingredients in separate bowl. Add and mix until moistened. Spoon 1/2 batter into greased and floured 10 inch (25 cm) angel food tube pan or bundt pan.

Sprinkle with half of chocolate chips. Spoon remaining batter over top. Sprinkle with second 1/2 chocolate chips. Bake in 350°F (175°C) oven for about 65 to 70 minutes. A wooden pick inserted in center should come out clean. Let stand for 30 minutes before turning out on rack to cool.

Spread with topping. Cuts into 16 wedges.

1 wedge: 421 Calories; 5 g Protein; 21.3 g Total Fat; 56 g Carbohydrate; 250 mg Sodium; 3 g Dietary Fiber

Pictured on page 39.

Chocolate Date Cake

A sugared nut and chip topping makes this cake company special. Ice sides, if desired, but top will "stand alone."

Boiling water	1 1/2 cups	375 mL
Chopped dates	1 cup	250 mL
Baking soda	1 tsp.	5 mL
Hard margarine, softened	3/4 cup	175 mL
Granulated sugar	1 cup	250 mL
Large egg	1	1
Vanilla	1 tsp.	5 mL
All-purpose flour	2 cups	500 mL
Cocoa, sifted	1 tbsp.	15 mL
Baking powder	2 tsp.	10 mL
Salt	1/2 tsp.	2 mL
Granulated sugar	1/4 cup	60 mL
Chopped walnuts	1/4 cup	60 mL
Semisweet chocolate chips	1/2 cup	125 mL
Chocolate Cheese Icing, page 111		

Pour boiling water over dates and baking soda in medium bowl. Let stand.

Cream margarine and first amount of sugar in large bowl. Beat in egg and vanilla.

Stir flour, cocoa, baking powder and salt in separate bowl. Add flour mixture in 3 additions, alternately with date mixture in 2 additions, beginning and ending with flour mixture. Turn into greased and floured 10 inch (25 cm) angel food tube pan.

Sprinkle with second amount of sugar, walnuts and chocolate chips. Bake in 350°F (175°C) oven for about 45 minutes. Cool completely before removing cake.

Ice sides only. Cuts into 16 wedges.

1 wedge: 271 Calories; 3 g Protein; 12.2 g Total Fat; 40 g Carbohydrate; 281 mg Sodium; 2 g Dietary Fiber

Pictured on page 39.

Top and Bottom: Pumpkin Chip Cake, this page
Center: Chocolate Date Cake, above

Chocolate Jelly Roll

For a simple look, dust roll with icing sugar or, to dress up, ice with whipped topping.

Large eggs	**4**	**4**
Granulated sugar	**2/3 cup**	**150 mL**
Vanilla	**1/2 tsp.**	**2 mL**
All-purpose flour	**3/4 cup**	**175 mL**
Cocoa, sifted	**1/3 cup**	**75 mL**
Warm water	**4 tsp.**	**20 mL**

Filling:
Chocolate Butter Icing, page 109

Combine eggs, sugar and vanilla in medium bowl. Beat well until thick enough to leave trail when beaters are lifted. Should be thick and mousse-like.

Sift flour and cocoa onto plate. Add to batter. Fold in. Add water. Fold together. Turn into greased and waxed paper-lined 10 × 15 inch (25 × 38 cm) jelly roll pan. Bake in 400°F (205°C) oven for 10 to 12 minutes. A wooden pick inserted in center should come out clean. Turn out onto tea towel dusted with icing sugar. Remove waxed paper. Trim crisp edges. Roll up from short end with towel.

Filling: Unroll when cool. Spread with icing to edges. Roll up without towel. Cuts into 12 slices.

1 slice: 292 Calories; 4 g Protein; 14.2 g Total Fat; 40 g Carbohydrate; 146 mg Sodium; 2 g Dietary Fiber

Pictured on page 40/41.

Chocolate Pound Cake

Moist and dense. Serve with a scoop of ice cream.

Hard margarine, softened	**1 cup**	**250 mL**
Granulated sugar	**2 cups**	**500 mL**
Large eggs	**4**	**4**
Vanilla	**1 tsp.**	**5 mL**
All-purpose flour	**2¼ cups**	**560 mL**
Cocoa, sifted	**⅓ cup**	**75 mL**
Baking soda	**1½ tsp.**	**7 mL**
Salt	**½ tsp.**	**2 mL**
Buttermilk (or reconstituted from powder)	**⅔ cup**	**150 mL**
Chocolate Icing, page 110, thinned to barely pourable consistency		

Cream margarine and sugar in large bowl. Beat in eggs, 1 at a time. Add vanilla. Mix.

Stir flour, cocoa, baking soda and salt in medium bowl.

Add flour mixture in 3 parts, alternately with buttermilk in 2 parts, beginning and ending with flour mixture. Turn into greased and floured 12 cup (2.7 L) bundt pan. Bake in 325°F (160°C) oven for about 1¼ hours. A wooden pick inserted in center should come out clean. Let stand for 20 minutes. Turn out cake to cool.

Spread icing over top, allowing some to run down sides. Cuts into 16 wedges.

1 wedge: 578 Calories; 5 g Protein; 22.6 g Total Fat; 93 g Carbohydrate; 461 mg Sodium; 2 g Dietary Fiber

Pictured on page 43.

Cheesy Cupcakes

No icing needed. The cheesy topping does it all.

Light cream cheese, softened	**8 oz.**	**250 g**
Granulated sugar	**½ cup**	**125 mL**
Large egg	**1**	**1**
Semisweet chocolate chips	**1 cup**	**250 mL**
All-purpose flour	**1½ cups**	**375 mL**
Granulated sugar	**1 cup**	**250 mL**
Cocoa, sifted	**⅓ cup**	**75 mL**
Baking soda	**1 tsp.**	**5 mL**
Salt	**½ tsp.**	**2 mL**
Hard margarine, softened	**6 tbsp.**	**100 mL**
Warm water	**1 cup**	**250 mL**
Vanilla	**1 tsp.**	**5 mL**

Beat cream cheese, sugar and egg in small bowl until smooth. Add chocolate chips. Stir. Set aside.

Measure next 5 ingredients into large bowl. Stir. Make a well.

Add margarine, water and vanilla to well. Beat for about 2 minutes until smooth. Line 20 muffin cups with paper liners. Fill with 2 tbsp. (30 mL) batter each. Spoon about 1 tbsp. (15 mL) cream cheese mixture over top. Bake in 350°F (175°C) oven for 30 to 35 minutes. Makes 20 cupcakes.

1 cupcake: 199 Calories; 3 g Protein; 8.7 g Total Fat; 29 g Carbohydrate; 301 mg Sodium; 2 g Dietary Fiber

Pictured on page 43.

Top Left: Smooth Chocolate Sauce, page 153
Top Right: Chocolate Pound Cake, page 42
Bottom: Cheesy Cupcakes, page 42

Chocolate Hazelnut Cake

Hazelnut flavor complemented by a mocha filling. An awesome cake.

Cake:		
Large eggs	**6**	**6**
Hazelnuts (filberts)	**1½ cups**	**375 mL**
Granulated sugar	**1 cup**	**250 mL**
Semisweet chocolate chips	**½ cup**	**125 mL**
Baking powder	**4 tsp.**	**20 mL**
Vanilla	**1 tsp.**	**5 mL**
Salt	**¼ tsp.**	**1 mL**
Filling:		
Hard margarine, softened	**2 tbsp.**	**30 mL**
Icing (confectioner's) sugar	**1 cup**	**250 mL**
Cocoa, sifted	**1 tsp.**	**5 mL**
Vanilla	**½ tsp.**	**2 mL**
Strong coffee	**2 tbsp.**	**30 mL**

Mocha Fluff Icing, page 110

Cake: Place all 7 ingredients in blender. Process for 3 minutes. Pour into 2 greased and waxed paper-lined 8 inch (20 cm) round cake layer pans. Bake in 350°F (175°C) oven for about 25 minutes until wooden pick inserted in center comes out clean. Cool.

Filling: Beat margarine, icing sugar, cocoa, vanilla and coffee together well in small bowl. Remove 1 cake layer, top side up, to plate. Spread with filling. Set second cake layer over filling, top side up.

Ice cake. Cuts into 12 rich wedges.

1 wedge: 347 Calories; 7 g Protein; 19.3 g Total Fat; 40 g Carbohydrate; 138 mg Sodium; 2 g Dietary Fiber

Pictured on page 45.

White Chocolate Pound Cake

Good choice for a cake. Instead of icing, simply dust with icing sugar.

White chocolate baking squares (1 oz., 28 g, each), cut up	**4**	**4**
Skim evaporated milk	**1 cup**	**250 mL**
Hard margarine, softened	**1 cup**	**250 mL**
Granulated sugar	**1⅔ cups**	**400 mL**
Large eggs	**5**	**5**
All-purpose flour	**2¾ cups**	**675 mL**
Baking soda	**½ tsp.**	**2 mL**
Salt	**½ tsp.**	**2 mL**

White Chocolate Icing, page 112 (½ recipe)

Combine chocolate and evaporated milk in medium saucepan. Heat on low, stirring often, until smooth. Cool to room temperature.

Cream margarine and sugar in large bowl. Beat in eggs, 1 at a time.

Stir flour, baking soda and salt in separate bowl. Add to batter in 3 parts, alternately with chocolate mixture in 2 parts, beginning and ending with flour mixture. Pour into greased and floured 12 cup (2.7 L) bundt pan. Bake in 325°F (160°C) oven for about 1 hour. A wooden pick inserted in center should come out clean. Let stand for 20 minutes. Turn out of pan to cool.

Ice cake. Cuts into 16 wedges.

1 wedge: 381 Calories; 7 g Protein; 17.9 g Total Fat; 49 g Carbohydrate; 321 mg Sodium; 1 g Dietary Fiber

Pictured on page 45.

Top: Chocolate Hazelnut Cake, this page
Bottom: White Chocolate Pound Cake, above

Last Minute Torte

This is perfect to make at the last minute. Easy to assemble.

Frozen pound cake, thawed	**14 oz.**	**390 g**
Fudge Icing, page 110		
Sliced or slivered almonds, toasted	**1 cup**	**250 mL**

Cut pound cake into 5 layers while partially frozen.

Spread ¼ cup (60 mL) icing over top of each layer. Sprinkle each layer with ⅙ of almonds, pressing to ensure they are secured. Assemble layers as you go. Spread remaining chocolate mixture over sides. Press remaining almonds on sides. Cuts into 10 slices.

1 slice: 359 Calories; 5 g Protein; 25.6 g Total Fat; 30 g Carbohydrate; 53 mg Sodium; 2 g Dietary Fiber

Pictured below.

Left: Last Minute Torte, above
Center: Sacher Torte, page 47 (garnished with chocolate leaves, page 21, and dried apricots)
Right: Fat-Free Chocolate Cake, this page (garnished with dusting of icing sugar, using a doily for the pattern)

Fat-Free Chocolate Cake

Totally amazing. Be sure to try it.
Dust with icing sugar, if desired.

All-purpose flour	**1¼ cups**	**300 mL**
Granulated sugar	**1 cup**	**250 mL**
Cocoa, sifted	**½ cup**	**125 mL**
Cornstarch	**¼ cup**	**60 mL**
Baking soda	**½ tsp.**	**2 mL**
Salt	**½ tsp.**	**2 mL**
Egg whites (large)	**4**	**4**
Water	**1 cup**	**250 mL**
Dark corn syrup	**½ cup**	**125 mL**

Measure first 6 ingredients into medium bowl. Stir. Make a well.

Place egg whites, water and corn syrup in separate medium bowl. Whisk to mix. Pour into well. Stir until smooth. Turn into greased 9 x 9 inch (22 x 22 cm) pan. Bake in 350°F (175°C) oven for about 30 minutes until wooden pick inserted in center comes out clean. Cuts into 16 pieces.

1 piece: 138 Calories; 3 g Protein; 0.3 g Total Fat; 33 g Carbohydrate; 149 mg Sodium; 2 g Dietary Fiber

Pictured on page 47.

Sacher Torte

In Austria this is served topped with whipped cream.

Semisweet chocolate baking squares (1 oz., 28 g, each), cut up	**5**	**5**
Hard margarine	**1 tbsp.**	**15 mL**
Hard margarine, softened	**½ cup**	**125 mL**
Granulated sugar	**½ cup**	**125 mL**
Egg yolks (large)	**5**	**5**
Vanilla	**1 tsp.**	**5 mL**
Cocoa, sifted	**2 tbsp.**	**30 mL**
All-purpose flour	**¾ cup**	**175 mL**
Salt	**¼ tsp.**	**1 mL**
Egg whites (large), room temperature	**5**	**5**
Apricot jam, heated and sieved	**1 cup**	**250 mL**
Chocolate Glaze, page 23		

Melt chocolate and first amount of margarine in medium saucepan on low, stirring constantly, until smooth. Cool to room temperature.

Cream second amount of margarine and sugar in medium bowl. Beat in egg yolks and vanilla until light and fluffy. Add chocolate to egg yolk mixture. Beat to blend.

Sift cocoa into flour and salt in small bowl. Stir into chocolate mixture.

Beat egg whites with clean beaters in large bowl until stiff. Fold into chocolate mixture in 4 additions. Turn into greased 9 inch (22 cm) springform pan. Bake in 350°F (175°C) oven for about 35 minutes. A wooden pick inserted in center should come out clean. Cool.

Cut cake into 2 layers. Spread bottom layer with scant ½ apricot jam. Add top layer. Spread remaining jam over top and sides. Let stand 1 hour or more to dry slightly.

Pour glaze over top and down sides of cake. Cuts into 12 wedges.

1 wedge: 389 Calories; 5 g Protein; 21.8 g Total Fat; 48 g Carbohydrate; 231 mg Sodium; 2 g Dietary Fiber

Pictured on page 46/47.

Jelly Roll Cake

No doubt you will be asked how you did this. Each slice has several rows of cake in it. A conversation piece.

Large eggs, room temperature	**8**	**8**
Granulated sugar	**1½ cups**	**375 mL**
Water	**¼ cup**	**60 mL**
Vanilla	**2 tsp.**	**10 mL**
Cake flour, sift before measuring	**1½ cups**	**375 mL**
Baking powder	**2 tsp.**	**10 mL**
Salt	**½ tsp.**	**2 mL**
Icing (confectioner's) sugar, sprinkle		
Chocolate Caramel Filling, page 113		

Grease two 10 x 15 inch (25 x 38 cm) jelly roll pans. Line with greased waxed paper. Beat eggs in large bowl until smooth. Add sugar. Beat until light-colored and thick.

Add water and vanilla. Stir.

Sift flour, baking powder and salt over batter. Fold in. Divide batter evenly between prepared pans. Bake, 1 pan at a time, in 400°F (205°C) oven for 12 to 15 minutes. A wooden pick inserted in center should come out clean. Cool cakes enough to handle. Sift icing sugar onto 2 tea towels. Turn out cakes onto towels. Roll cakes up from narrow end, with towels.

To Assemble: Unroll jelly rolls. Using a ruler, cut each into 3 lengthwise portions of equal width. Spread each cake strip with ⅓ cup (75 mL) filling. Carefully roll up 1 strip like jelly roll. Set roll on cut edge on plate. Wind second strip around roll, beginning where first strip ended. Repeat with 4 remaining strips. Ice top and sides of cake with remaining icing. Chill. Cuts into 16 wedges.

1 wedge: 231 Calories; 5 g Protein; 5.7 g Total Fat; 41 g Carbohydrate; 175 mg Sodium; 1 g Dietary Fiber

Pictured on page 49.

Chocolate Cake

A rich, glossy icing makes this cake special. Good texture. Moist and chocolaty.

Unsweetened chocolate baking squares (1 oz., 28 g, each), cut up	**3**	**3**
Boiling water	**1 cup**	**250 mL**
Hard margarine, softened	**½ cup**	**125 mL**
Granulated sugar	**1½ cups**	**375 mL**
Large eggs	**3**	**3**
Vanilla	**1 tsp.**	**5 mL**
All-purpose flour	**2¼ cups**	**560 mL**
Baking soda	**1½ tsp.**	**7 mL**
Salt	**½ tsp.**	**2 mL**
Sour cream	**1 cup**	**250 mL**
Sour Cream Icing, page 112		
Fudge Icing, page 110		

Place chocolate in medium bowl. Add boiling water. Stir until chocolate is melted. Cool to room temperature.

Cream margarine and sugar in large bowl. Beat in eggs, 1 at a time. Add vanilla. Mix.

Stir flour, baking soda and salt in separate medium bowl.

Mix in flour mixture in 3 parts, alternately with sour cream in 2 parts. Add chocolate mixture. Stir. Turn into 2 greased 8 inch (20 cm) round layer cake pans. Bake in 350°F (175°C) oven for about 35 to 40 minutes. A wooden pick inserted in center should come out clean. Cool.

Spread Sour Cream Icing over top and sides. Pipe with Fudge Icing and remaining Sour Cream Icing. Cuts into 12 wedges.

1 wedge: 605 Calories; 6 g Protein; 25.9 g Total Fat; 92 g Carbohydrate; 458 mg Sodium; 3 g Dietary Fiber

Pictured on page 49.

Top and Bottom: Jelly Roll Cake, this page
Center: Chocolate Cake, above

Chocolate candies, bonbons, fudge and nuts—every child's dream come true—have been neatly wrapped and delivered in this selection of recipes. Making handmade chocolate candies is an event to be savored—the anticipation as it cooks, the wonderful aroma that creeps through every room in the house and the inevitable beckoning of the sticky pot, spoon or spatula. Gather the children together and let them in on a memorable experience. Wrap your candies in brightly colored foil or boxes and present them as a gift to your favorite aunt, neighbor or sweetheart. Nothing is more appreciated than homemade chocolate candy!

Candy

Frosty Bananas

Use the leftover chocolate in Fruit And Nut Clusters, page 14.

Popsicle sticks	**8**	**8**
Bananas, firm and slightly underripe, cut in half crosswise	**4**	**4**
Semisweet chocolate baking squares (1 oz., 28 g, each)	**8**	**8**
Coatings (such as chocolate sprinkles, rainbow sprinkles or crushed nuts), optional		

Push a popsicle stick lengthwise, about 2 inches (5 cm) into each banana half.

Slowly melt chocolate over hot water, or in saucepan on low, stirring constantly, until smooth. Do not overheat. Pour into tall drinking glass, about 2/3 full. Holding popsicle stick, lower banana into chocolate until completely covered. Gently rotate and pull banana out, letting excess chocolate drip back into glass. Immediately roll in desired topping. Place on waxed paper on baking sheet. Freeze, uncovered, until solid. Place frozen bananas in airtight container. Return to freezer. Makes 8.

1 covered banana (without coating): 195 Calories; 2 g Protein; 10.3 g Total Fat; 29 g Carbohydrate; 4 mg Sodium; 3 g Dietary Fiber

Pictured on this page.

Chocolate Marshmallows

Allow extra time for this impressive-looking candy dessert. Certainly worth the time it takes.

Can of sweetened condensed milk	**11 oz.**	**300 mL**
Jar of marshmallow crème	**7 oz.**	**200 g**
Semisweet chocolate chips	**2⅓ cups**	**575 mL**
Large marshmallows	**60**	**60**
Finely chopped walnuts (or pecans)	**4½ cups**	**1.1 L**

Combine condensed milk, marshmallow crème and chocolate chips in medium saucepan. Heat on low, stirring often, until smooth. Remove from heat. Reheat if mixture becomes too thick for dipping.

Drop 1 marshmallow at a time into chocolate. Use 2 forks to roll and coat. Lift marshmallow with fork and drop into chopped walnuts in small bowl. Roll to coat. Cool on waxed paper overnight. Makes 60.

1 coated marshmallow: 146 Calories; 2 g Protein; 8.8 g Total Fat; 17 g Carbohydrate; 18 mg Sodium; 1 g Dietary Fiber

Pictured on page 53.

Chocolate Nuts

These are a pleasant change from the usual mixed nut offering.

Pecan halves	**1 cup**	**250 mL**
Walnut halves	**1 cup**	**250 mL**
Cooking oil	**4 tsp.**	**20 mL**
Chocolate Syrup, page 174	**½ cup**	**125 mL**

Combine pecans and walnuts in medium bowl. Add cooking oil and chocolate syrup. Stir well. Spread in large greased baking pan. Bake in 350°F (175°C) oven for 8 to 10 minutes, stirring at half-time, until dry and crisp. Makes 2 cups (500 mL).

2 tbsp. (30 mL): 124 Calories; 2 g Protein; 10.3 g Total Fat; 9 g Carbohydrate; 6 mg Sodium; 1 g Dietary Fiber

Pictured on page 53.

Brittle lovers, take note. Lots of peanuts and covered in chocolate. A dream come true.

Granulated sugar	**1 cup**	**250 mL**
White corn syrup	**½ cup**	**125 mL**
Roasted salted peanuts	**1 cup**	**250 mL**
Hard margarine	**2 tbsp.**	**30 mL**
Vanilla	**1 tsp.**	**5 mL**
Baking soda	**1½ tsp.**	**7 mL**
Topping:		
Semisweet chocolate chips	**¾ cup**	**175 mL**
Chopped peanuts (or pecans)	**¼ cup**	**60 mL**

Combine sugar and corn syrup in 2 quart (2 L) casserole. Microwave, uncovered, on high (100%) for 4 minutes.

Stir in peanuts. Microwave, uncovered, on high (100%) for about 6 minutes, checking at 1 minute intervals, until golden.

Add margarine and vanilla. Stir. Microwave, uncovered, on high (100%) for 1 minute.

Stir in baking soda. While still foamy, pour and spread thinly on greased baking sheet.

Topping: Sprinkle chocolate chips over top. When softened, spread over all. Sprinkle with chopped peanuts. Chill thoroughly. Break into pieces. Makes about 1¼ lbs. (560 g).

¼ lb. (113 g): 638 Calories; 10 g Protein; 31.1 g Total Fat; 89 g Carbohydrate; 796 mg Sodium; 5 g Dietary Fiber

Pictured on page 53.

Top Left: Chocolate Nuts, this page
Top Right: Chocolate Marshmallows, this page
Bottom: Chocolate Brittle, above

White Chocolate Fudge

Serve chilled. Creamy with pecans throughout. Drizzle with melted chocolate.

Cream cheese, softened	**8 oz.**	**250 g**
Icing (confectioner's) sugar	**4 cups**	**1 L**
White chocolate baking squares (1 oz., 28 g, each), cut up	**12**	**12**
Vanilla	**1½ tsp.**	**7 mL**
Ground pecans	**⅔ cup**	**150 mL**

Beat cream cheese and icing sugar in large bowl, adding sugar 1 cup (250 mL) at a time.

Melt chocolate in large saucepan over hot water, or on low, stirring constantly, until smooth. Do not overheat. Stir into cream cheese mixture.

Add vanilla and pecans. Stir. Spread in greased 8 × 8 inch (20 × 20 cm) pan. Chill. Cuts into 64 squares.

1 square: 80 Calories; 1 g Protein; 3.8 g Total Fat; 11 g Carbohydrate; 16 mg Sodium; trace Dietary Fiber

Pictured on page 55.

Kona Truffles

A real chocolate flavor coated in coconut. Sinful!

Semisweet chocolate chips	**2 cups**	**500 mL**
Can of sweetened condensed milk	**11 oz.**	**300 mL**
Vanilla	**1 tsp.**	**5 mL**
Chopped walnuts	**¾ cup**	**175 mL**
Medium coconut, plain or toasted	**1 cup**	**250 mL**

Melt chocolate chips in medium saucepan over hot water, or on low, stirring constantly, until smooth. Do not overheat. Remove from heat.

Add condensed milk, vanilla and walnuts. Stir well. Chill several hours or overnight.

With greased hands, shape into 1 inch (2.5 cm) balls. Roll in coconut to coat. Chill. Makes 48.

1 truffle: 84 Calories; 1 g Protein; 5.5 g Total Fat; 9 g Carbohydrate; 12 mg Sodium; 1 g Dietary Fiber

Pictured on page 55.

Chocolate Pralines

Very sweet, chocolaty and nutty.

Granulated sugar	**1½ cups**	**375 mL**
Brown sugar, packed	**1½ cups**	**375 mL**
Evaporated milk	**1 cup**	**250 mL**
Salt	**½ tsp.**	**2 mL**
Unsweetened chocolate baking squares (1 oz., 28 g, each), cut up	**2**	**2**
Hard margarine	**2 tbsp.**	**30 mL**
Vanilla	**1 tsp.**	**5 mL**
Chopped pecans	**2 cups**	**500 mL**

Combine first 4 ingredients in large heavy saucepan. Heat on medium, stirring constantly, until mixture comes to a boil. Stir until soft ball stage (about 234°F, 112°C, on candy thermometer) or until small amount dropped into very cold water forms a soft pliable ball. Remove from heat.

Add chocolate, margarine, vanilla and pecans. Stir until starting to thicken. Quickly drop small spoonfuls onto waxed paper. If mixture becomes too thick to drop, reheat slightly. Makes 3 dozen.

1 praline: 140 Calories; 1 g Protein; 6.8 g Total Fat; 21 g Carbohydrate; 56 mg Sodium; 1 g Dietary Fiber

Pictured on page 55.

Top Left: White Chocolate Fudge, this page (with and without chocolate drizzle, page 22)
Center Right: Chocolate Pralines, above
Bottom: Kona Truffles, this page

Chocolate Crunch

Plan to make lots of this! Even if you hide it, it's sure to be found. Use any leftover melted chocolate in Fruit And Nut Clusters, page 14.

Smooth peanut butter	**½ cup**	**125 mL**
Dark corn syrup	**¼ cup**	**60 mL**
Crisp rice cereal	**½ cup**	**125 mL**
Coating:		
Semisweet chocolate baking squares (1 oz., 28 g, each), cut up	**4**	**4**

Mix peanut butter and corn syrup well in small bowl. Add rice cereal. Work together. Shape into log 1¼ inches (3 cm) diameter and about 8 inches (20 cm) long. Chill. Cut with sharp knife into ¼ inch (6 mm) slices.

Coating: Melt chocolate in small saucepan over hot water, or on low, stirring often, until smooth. Do not overheat. Dip slice, pierced on fork, into chocolate, allowing excess to drip back into saucepan. Place on waxed paper to harden. Makes 32.

1 slice: 52 Calories; 1 g Protein; 3.4 g Total Fat; 5 g Carbohydrate; 25 mg Sodium; trace Dietary Fiber

Pictured on page 57.

Bavarian Mints

Serve these chocolate minty-flavored goodies after dessert with a second cup of coffee.

Semisweet chocolate chips	**1 cup**	**250 mL**
Unsweetened chocolate baking square, cut up	**1 oz.**	**28 g**
Hard margarine	**1½ tsp.**	**7 mL**
Sweetened condensed milk	**⅓ cup**	**75 mL**
Peppermint flavoring	**¼ tsp.**	**1 mL**
Icing (confectioner's) sugar	**⅓ cup**	**75 mL**
Icing (confectioner's) sugar, for garnish		

Melt chocolate chips, chocolate square and margarine in medium saucepan over hot water, or on low, stirring constantly, until smooth. Do not overheat. Remove from heat.

Add condensed milk, peppermint flavoring and icing sugar. Mix well. Work with hands until pliable. Divide dough into portions. Work each portion into ½ inch (12 mm) thick rope. Cut with sharp knife into ½ inch (12 mm) pieces. Place on waxed paper to set.

Sieve icing sugar over top. Makes about 8 dozen.

1 mint: 15 Calories; trace Protein; 0.9 g Total Fat; 2 g Carbohydrate; 2 mg Sodium; trace Dietary Fiber

Pictured on page 57.

Top: Chocolate Crunch, this page
Bottom: Bavarian Mints, above

Chocolate Cherry Fudge

This will remind you of chocolate-covered cherries. Store in refrigerator.

Granulated sugar	**3 cups**	**750 mL**
Light cream	**1 cup**	**250 mL**
Unsweetened chocolate baking squares (1 oz., 28 g, each), cut up	**3**	**3**
Corn syrup	**2 tbsp.**	**30 mL**
Hard margarine	**2 tbsp.**	**30 mL**
Salt	**⅛ tsp.**	**0.5 mL**
Vanilla	**1 tsp.**	**5 mL**
Maraschino cherries, well drained and chopped	**½ cup**	**125 mL**

Combine first 6 ingredients in 3 quart (3 L) saucepan. Heat on low, stirring constantly, until sugar is dissolved. Bring mixture to a boil. Boil slowly until soft ball stage (about 234°F, 112°C, on candy thermometer) or until small amount dropped into very cold water forms a soft pliable ball. Remove from heat. Let stand for 40 minutes to cool slightly.

Add vanilla. Beat until mixture loses its gloss and starts to thicken. Quickly add cherries. Pour into greased 8 × 8 inch (20 × 20 cm) pan. Cool. Cuts into 36 pieces.

1 piece: 100 Calories; trace Protein; 2.7 g Total Fat; 20 g Carbohydrate; 22 mg Sodium; trace Dietary Fiber

Pictured on page 59.

Chocolate Fudge

Creamy smooth. Because it's so thick, cut into small squares. For a special touch, drizzle individual pieces with melted white chocolate.

Semisweet chocolate chips	**2 cups**	**500 mL**
Milk chocolate chips	**2 cups**	**500 mL**
Jar of marshmallow crème	**7 oz.**	**200 g**
Chopped pecans (or walnuts)	**½ cup**	**125 mL**
Can of evaporated milk	**13½ oz.**	**385 mL**
Granulated sugar	**4½ cups**	**1.1 L**
Hard margarine	**2 tbsp.**	**30 mL**
Salt, just a pinch		

Combine first 4 ingredients in large bowl. Set aside.

Place evaporated milk, sugar, margarine and salt in medium saucepan. Heat, stirring occasionally, until boiling. Boil, stirring constantly, for 5 minutes. Pour over chips in bowl. Stir until mixed well and chips are melted. Turn into greased 9 × 9 inch (22 × 22 cm) pan. Chill thoroughly. Cuts into 144 pieces.

1 piece: 61 Calories; 1 g Protein; 2.2 g Total Fat; 11 g Carbohydrate; 8 mg Sodium; trace Dietary Fiber

Pictured on page 59.

Top Left and Bottom: Chocolate Cherry Fudge, this page
Top Right: Chocolate Fudge, above

Cheesecakes

See if you can find the smooth flavor of chocolate in these bold cheesecake concoctions. It could be hiding in the crust, peeking out from inside the cheese, or revealing itself in swirls atop your dessert.

These recipes feature both spectacular presentations and sophisticated flavors. Can you even begin to imagine what heavenly taste is waiting tucked inside a Turtle Cheesecake, or what delights await in a slice of Black Forest Cheesecake? The answer can be found with the turn of a page.

Mini Chip Cheesecakes

Smooth and creamy with lots of little chocolate bits. Garnish with whipped topping and Chocolate Filigrees, page 24, just before serving.

Chocolate wafers	**12**	**12**
Light cream cheese (8 oz., 250 g, each), softened	**2**	**2**
Granulated sugar	**3/4 cup**	**175 mL**
Large eggs	**2**	**2**
Vanilla	**1 tsp.**	**5 mL**
Mini semisweet chocolate chips	**1/2 cup**	**125 mL**
Mini semisweet chocolate chips	**1/2 cup**	**125 mL**

Line ungreased muffin cups with large paper liners. Place 1 wafer in bottom of each liner.

Beat cream cheese and sugar in medium bowl until smooth. Beat in eggs, 1 at a time, on low just until blended. Add vanilla. Mix in.

Melt first amount of chocolate chips in small saucepan over hot water, or on low, stirring constantly, until smooth. Do not overheat. Add to batter.

Add second amount of chocolate chips. Fold in. Divide over wafers. Bake in 325°F (160°C) oven for 25 to 30 minutes until set. Cool, then chill. Makes 12.

1 cheesecake: 275 Calories; 7 g Protein; 15.2 g Total Fat; 31 g Carbohydrate; 462 mg Sodium; 1 g Dietary Fiber

Pictured on this page.

Mocha Cheesecake Freeze

A freezer dessert that can be served without thawing.

Chocolate Wafer Crust:		
Hard margarine	1/4 cup	60 mL
Chocolate wafer crumbs	1 1/4 cups	300 mL
Brown sugar, packed	1/4 cup	60 mL
Filling:		
Cream cheese, softened	8 oz.	250 g
Can of sweetened condensed milk	11 oz.	300 mL
Instant coffee granules, rolled to a powder	1 tbsp.	15 mL
Semisweet chocolate chips	2/3 cup	150 mL
Water	3 tbsp.	50 mL
Envelope of dessert topping (not prepared)	1	1
Milk	1/2 cup	125 mL

Chocolate Wafer Crust: Melt margarine in medium saucepan. Stir in wafer crumbs and brown sugar. Reserve 2 tbsp. (30 mL). Press remaining crumb mixture into ungreased bottom and up side of 9 inch (22 cm) springform pan.

Filling: Beat cream cheese, condensed milk and coffee powder in large bowl until creamy and light.

Combine chocolate chips and water in small saucepan over hot water, or on low, stirring constantly, until smooth. Do not overheat. Set saucepan in cold water. Stir to hasten cooling. Beat into cream cheese mixture.

Beat topping mix and milk in small bowl until stiff. Fold into cream cheese mixture. Turn into prepared pan. Sprinkle with reserved crumbs. Freeze. Cuts into 12 wedges.

1 wedge: 354 Calories; 6 g Protein; 21.4 g Total Fat; 38 g Carbohydrate; 210 mg Sodium; 1 g Dietary Fiber

Pictured on page 63.

Cookie Cheesecake

Lots of dark flecks throughout. Very attractive—especially if garnished with whipped topping and whole cookies.

Crust:		
Hard margarine	2 tbsp.	30 mL
Crushed cream-filled chocolate cookies	1 1/2 cups	375 mL
Filling:		
Light cream cheese (8 oz., 250 g, each), softened	3	3
Granulated sugar	1 cup	250 mL
Vanilla	1 1/2 tsp.	7 mL
Whipping cream	1 cup	250 mL
Large eggs	3	3
Coarsely chopped cream-filled chocolate cookies	1 cup	250 mL

Crust: Melt margarine in medium saucepan. Stir in crushed cookies. Press in bottom and 1/2 inch (12 mm) up side of ungreased 10 inch (25 cm) springform pan.

Filling: Beat cream cheese, sugar and vanilla in large bowl until smooth. Beat in whipping cream. Beat in eggs, 1 at a time, on low until just blended.

Fold in chopped cookies. Turn into prepared pan. Bake in 325°F (160°C) oven for about 1 1/4 hours until center is set. Run paring knife around edge of pan to allow cake to settle evenly without cracking. Cool. Chill overnight. Cuts into 16 wedges.

1 wedge: 285 Calories; 7 g Protein; 18.1 g Total Fat; 24 g Carbohydrate; 541 mg Sodium; trace Dietary Fiber

Pictured on page 63.

1. Cookie Cheesecake, above
2. Mocha Cheesecake Freeze, this page (garnished with Fudge Icing, page 110)
3. Mini Chilled Cheesecakes, page 64

Mini Chilled Cheesecakes

Filling is soft, rich and mousse-like. A handy whole-wafer crust. No baking required. Garnish with whipped topping, pieces of fresh fruit, Chocolate Filigrees, page 24, or whatever you desire.

Chocolate wafers	**12**	**12**
Light cream cheese, softened	**8 oz.**	**250 g**
Granulated sugar	**1 cup**	**250 mL**
Cocoa, sifted	**1/3 cup**	**75 mL**
Vanilla	**1 tsp.**	**5 mL**
Envelope of unflavored gelatin	**1/4 oz.**	**7 g**
Water	**1/4 cup**	**60 mL**
Frozen light whipped topping, thawed	**2 cups**	**500 mL**

Line ungreased muffin cups with large paper liners. Place 1 wafer in bottom of each liner.

Beat cream cheese, sugar, cocoa and vanilla in large bowl until smooth.

Sprinkle gelatin over water in small saucepan. Let stand for 1 minute. Heat on medium, stirring constantly until dissolved. Set saucepan in cold water, stirring, until cooled to lukewarm. Beat into cream cheese mixture.

Fold in topping. Spoon over chocolate wafers. Chill until firm. Serves 12.

1 serving: 212 Calories; 4 g Protein; 8.5 g Total Fat; 33 g Carbohydrate; 256 mg Sodium; 2 g Dietary Fiber

Pictured on page 63.

Turtle Cheesecake

The ultimate! As decadent as it gets!

Crust:		
Hard margarine	**1/2 cup**	**125 mL**
Vanilla wafer crumbs	**2 cups**	**500 mL**
Second Layer:		
Caramels	**40**	**40**
Skim evaporated milk	**1/4 cup**	**60 mL**
Chopped pecans, toasted	**1 cup**	**250 mL**
Third Layer:		
Light cream cheese (8 oz., 250 g, each), softened	**2**	**2**
Granulated sugar	**1/2 cup**	**125 mL**
Vanilla	**1 tsp.**	**5 mL**
Large eggs	**2**	**2**
Semisweet chocolate chips	**1/2 cup**	**125 mL**
Chocolate Glaze, page 23		

Crust: Melt margarine in small saucepan. Add wafer crumbs. Stir well. Press in bottom and 1 inch (2.5 cm) up side of 9 inch (22 cm) springform pan. Bake in 350°F (175°C) oven for 5 minutes. Cool.

Second Layer: Heat caramels and evaporated milk in medium saucepan, stirring often, until smooth. Pour over crust.

Sprinkle with pecans.

Third Layer: Beat cream cheese, sugar and vanilla in large bowl until smooth. Beat in eggs on low, 1 at a time, just until blended.

Heat chocolate chips in small saucepan over hot water, or on low, stirring constantly, until smooth. Do not overheat. Stir into cream cheese mixture. Pour over pecans. Bake in 350°F (175°C) oven for 50 to 55 minutes. Run paring knife around edge of pan to allow cake to settle evenly without cracking. Cool.

Remove sides of pan. Place cake on rack set on waxed paper. Pour glaze over top and down sides of cake. Cuts into 12 wedges.

1 wedge: 585 Calories; 8 g Protein; 37.4 g Total Fat; 60 g Carbohydrate; 443 mg Sodium; 2 g Dietary Fiber

Pictured on page 65.

Turtle Cheesecake, page 64
(garnished with whipped topping, dipped whole pecans and spun sugar)

Mochaccino Cheesecake

Indulge in this impressive dessert. Freezes well.

Crust:		
Hard margarine	1/3 cup	75 mL
Graham cracker crumbs	1 1/3 cups	325 mL
Granulated sugar	1/3 cup	75 mL
Cocoa, sifted	3 tbsp.	50 mL
Filling:		
Semisweet chocolate baking squares (1 oz., 28 g, each), cut up	3	3
Cream cheese (8 oz., 250 g, each), softened	3	3
Granulated sugar	1/2 cup	125 mL
Brown sugar, packed	1/2 cup	125 mL
All-purpose flour	2 tbsp.	30 mL
Coffee liqueur (or vanilla)	2 tsp.	10 mL
Large eggs, room temperature	3	3
Milk	1/4 cup	60 mL
Instant coffee granules	1 tbsp.	15 mL

Crust: Melt margarine in small saucepan. Stir in crumbs, sugar and cocoa. Press in bottom of ungreased 9 inch (22 cm) springform pan. Set aside.

Filling: Melt chocolate in small saucepan over hot water, or on low, stirring constantly, until smooth. Do not overheat. Cool to room temperature.

Beat cream cheese, both sugars, flour and liqueur in medium bowl. Beat in melted chocolate. Beat in eggs, 1 at a time, just until mixed.

Stir milk and coffee granules in cup to dissolve coffee. Mix into batter. Pour over crust in pan. Bake in 300°F (150°C) oven for about 1 1/2 hours until center is almost set. Run paring knife around edge of pan to allow cake to settle evenly without cracking. Cool. Chill for 8 hours or overnight. Cuts into 12 wedges.

1 wedge: 476 Calories; 8 g Protein; 32.4 g Total Fat; 42 g Carbohydrate; 356 mg Sodium; 1 g Dietary Fiber

Pictured on page 67.

Chocolate Amaretto Cheesecake

Garnish with Amaretto-flavored whipped topping and chocolate-dipped whole almonds for a lavish presentation.

Crust:		
Hard margarine	1/4 cup	60 mL
Granulated sugar	3 tbsp.	50 mL
Graham cracker crumbs	1 1/4 cups	300 mL
Cocoa, sifted	3 tbsp.	50 mL
Filling:		
Semisweet chocolate baking squares (1 oz., 28 g, each), cut up	6	6
Cream cheese (8 oz., 250 g, each), softened	2	2
Granulated sugar	1/2 cup	125 mL
Large eggs	2	2
Sour cream	2/3 cup	150 mL
Amaretto liqueur	1/3 cup	75 mL
Vanilla	1 tsp.	5 mL
Almond flavoring	1/2 tsp.	2 mL

Crust: Melt margarine in saucepan. Stir in sugar, graham crumbs and cocoa. Press in bottom and 1 inch (2.5 cm) up side of ungreased 9 inch (22 cm) springform pan. Chill.

Filling: Melt chocolate in small saucepan over hot water, or on low, stirring constantly, until smooth. Do not overheat.

Beat cream cheese and sugar well in medium bowl. Beat in eggs, 1 at a time, just until blended. Stir in remaining 4 ingredients. Stir in melted chocolate. Pour filling over crust. Bake in 300°F (150°C) oven for 1 hour. Turn oven off. Do not open oven door. Leave cheesecake in oven for 1 more hour. Cool. Chill overnight. Cuts into 12 wedges.

1 wedge: 484 Calories; 8 g Protein; 32.5 g Total Fat; 41 g Carbohydrate; 324 mg Sodium; 2 g Dietary Fiber

Pictured on page 67.

Top: Mochaccino Cheesecake, this page (garnished with Chocolate Whipped Topping, page 109, and chocolate drizzle, page 22, broken)
Bottom: Chocolate Amaretto Cheesecake, above

Black Forest Cheesecake

A superb variation of Black Forest Cake.

Chocolate Wafer Crust:		
Hard margarine	1/3 cup	75 mL
Chocolate wafer crumbs	1 1/2 cups	375 mL
Granulated sugar	2 tbsp.	30 mL
Filling:		
Cream cheese (8 oz., 250 g, each), softened	4	4
Granulated sugar	1 1/2 cups	375 mL
Cocoa, sifted	1 cup	250 mL
Large eggs	4	4
Whipping cream	1 cup	250 mL
Vanilla	1 tsp.	5 mL
Maraschino cherries, well drained and finely chopped	1/2 cup	125 mL
Topping:		
Can of cherry pie filling	19 oz.	540 mL
Semisweet chocolate chips	1/3 cup	75 mL
Frozen light whipped topping, thawed	2 cups	500 mL

Chocolate Wafer Crust: Melt margarine in medium saucepan. Stir in wafer crumbs and sugar. Press in bottom of ungreased 10 inch (25 cm) springform pan. Chill.

Filling: Beat cream cheese and sugar in large bowl. Mix in cocoa. Beat in eggs, 1 at a time, on low. Add whipping cream and vanilla. Beat in slowly.

Fold in cherries. Pour over chilled crust. Bake in 325°F (160°C) oven for about 1 1/4 hours until center is almost set. Place on rack to cool. Immediately run paring knife around edge of pan to allow cake to settle evenly without cracking. Cool completely.

Topping: Spread cherry pie filling on cooled cake using as much as desired.

Melt chocolate chips in small saucepan over hot water, or on low, stirring constantly, until smooth. Do not overheat. Drizzle or pipe over pie filling. Spoon or pipe topping around outside edge. Chill. Cuts into 16 wedges.

1 wedge: 553 Calories; 9 g Protein; 37.6 g Total Fat; 51 g Carbohydrate; 300 mg Sodium; 3 g Dietary Fiber

Pictured on page 69.

Marble Cheesecake

Make one day or even two days ahead. Keep garnish around edges to show off marbling on top.

Crust:		
Hard margarine	6 tbsp.	100 mL
Graham cracker crumbs	1 1/2 cups	375 mL
Granulated sugar	2 tbsp.	30 mL
Cocoa, sifted	2 tbsp.	30 mL
Filling:		
Cream cheese (8 oz., 250 g, each), softened	3	3
Granulated sugar	1 cup	250 mL
All-purpose flour	3 tbsp.	50 mL
Large eggs	4	4
Vanilla	1 1/2 tsp.	7 mL
Whipping cream	1 cup	250 mL
Unsweetened chocolate baking squares (1 oz., 28 g, each), cut up	2	2

Crust: Melt margarine in small saucepan. Stir in graham crumbs, sugar and cocoa. Press in bottom of ungreased 9 inch (22 cm) springform pan. Bake in 350°F (175°C) oven for 10 minutes. Cool.

Filling: Beat cream cheese, sugar and flour in medium bowl until smooth.

Beat in eggs on low, 1 at a time. Add vanilla and whipping cream. Mix. Measure 1 1/2 cups (375 mL). Set aside. Pour remaining batter over crust.

Melt chocolate in small saucepan over hot water, or on low, stirring constantly, until smooth. Do not overheat. Cool. Stir into reserved batter. Spoon dabs over top of batter in pan. Using knife, cut zigzag pattern through batter. (See Marbling, page 23.) Bake in 350°F (175°C) oven for 1 hour until knife inserted off center comes out clean. Immediately run paring knife around edge of pan to allow cake to settle evenly without cracking. Cuts into 12 wedges.

1 wedge: 522 Calories; 9 g Protein; 39.8 g Total Fat; 36 g Carbohydrate; 376 mg Sodium; 2 g Dietary Fiber

Pictured on page 69.

Top: Black Forest Cheesecake, this page
Bottom: Marble Cheesecake, above
(garnished with Fudge Icing, page 110, and sliced almonds)

Cookies

Chocolate bonbons may be the traditional gesture of love on Valentine's Day, but there's hardly a person on earth who wouldn't also melt at the sight of homemade chocolate cookies, baked with love. But don't forget too, that any occasion to make cookies is a good occasion. After all, it's fun mixing the dough, sampling the dough, rolling out and decorating the dough. The process is fun, the anticipation is fun, the results, without a doubt, are doubly fun. And it's so easy to make twice the batch. Put your hand in the cookie jar—what will you find? A White Chip Cookie? Or a Chocolate Cherry Cookie? Or...?

Outer Circle: White Chip Cookies, page 72
Second Circle: Crispy Cookies, page 72
Inner Circle: Meringue Bites, page 72

Meringue Bites

Sweet nothings.

Egg whites (large), room temperature	2	2
Granulated sugar	2/3 cup	150 mL
Salt	1/8 tsp.	0.5 mL
Mini semisweet chocolate chips	2/3 cup	150 mL
Finely chopped walnuts (or pecans)	2/3 cup	150 mL
Cocoa, sifted	4 tsp.	20 mL
Vanilla	1 tsp.	5 mL

Beat egg whites in medium bowl until soft peaks form. Gradually add sugar and salt, beating until stiff.

Fold in chocolate chips, walnuts, cocoa and vanilla. Drop by teaspoonfuls onto greased baking sheet. Bake in 300°F (150°C) oven for about 20 minutes. Makes about 40.

1 meringue: 42 Calories; 1 g Protein; 2.3 g Total Fat; 5 g Carbohydrate; 12 mg Sodium; trace Dietary Fiber

Pictured on page 71.

Crispy Cookies

The secret to crispiness is the rolled oats.

Hard margarine, softened	3/4 cup	175 mL
Granulated sugar	1 cup	250 mL
Brown sugar, packed	1/2 cup	125 mL
Large egg	1	1
Vanilla	1 tsp.	5 mL
All-purpose flour	1 cup	250 mL
Quick-cooking rolled oats (not instant)	1 1/4 cups	300 mL
Cocoa, sifted	2 tbsp.	30 mL
Baking powder	3/4 tsp.	4 mL
Baking soda	3/4 tsp.	4 mL

Cream margarine and both sugars in large bowl. Beat in egg and vanilla.

Add remaining 5 ingredients. Mix well. Shape into 1 1/2 inch (3.8 cm) balls. Arrange on ungreased baking sheet. Bake in 375°F (190°C) oven for about 10 minutes. Makes 3 dozen.

1 cookie: 99 Calories; 1 g Protein; 4.5 g Total Fat; 14 g Carbohydrate; 80 mg Sodium; 1 g Dietary Fiber

Pictured on page 71.

White Chip Cookies

Rich chocolate flavor, fancy-looking and dramatic.

Hard margarine, softened	1/2 cup	125 mL
Brown sugar, packed	1 cup	250 mL
Cocoa, sifted	1/2 cup	125 mL
Large egg	1	1
Vanilla	1 tsp.	5 mL
All-purpose flour	1 cup	250 mL
Baking soda	1/2 tsp.	2 mL
Salt	1/2 tsp.	2 mL
White chocolate chips	1 cup	250 mL
Chopped walnuts (or pecans), optional	3/4 cup	175 mL

Cream margarine, brown sugar and cocoa in large bowl until smooth. Beat in egg and vanilla until fluffy.

Add remaining 5 ingredients. Mix well. Drop by rounded tablespoonfuls onto greased cookie sheet. Flatten slightly with fingers or glass. Bake in 350°F (175°C) oven for 10 to 12 minutes. Makes 3 dozen cookies.

1 cookie: 90 Calories; 1 g Protein; 4.3 g Total Fat; 12 g Carbohydrate; 96 mg Sodium; 1 g Dietary Fiber

Pictured on page 71.

Rum Balls

Add these to a plate of goodies. They also make a great gift.

Semisweet chocolate chips	**1 cup**	**250 mL**
Sour cream	**½ cup**	**125 mL**
Graham cracker (or vanilla wafer) crumbs	**3 cups**	**750 mL**
Icing (confectioner's) sugar	**½ cup**	**125 mL**
Corn syrup	**2 tbsp.**	**30 mL**
Rum flavoring	**2 tbsp.**	**30 mL**
Finely chopped pecans (or walnuts)	**1 cup**	**250 mL**
Coatings (such as granulated sugar, cocoa, ground hazelnuts, ground walnuts, chocolate sprinkles or ground pecans)		

Heat chocolate chips and sour cream in large saucepan on low, stirring often, until smooth.

Add next 5 ingredients. Mix well. Shape into 1 inch (2.5 cm) balls.

Roll balls in your choice of coating. Place in covered container. Chill. Makes about 78 balls.

1 ball: 45 Calories; 1 g Protein; 2.4 g Total Fat; 6 g Carbohydrate; 31 mg Sodium; 1 g Dietary Fiber

Pictured on this page.

Chocolate Chews

Nutty, soft-textured cookies.

Hard margarine, softened	½ cup	125 mL
Brown sugar, packed	1 cup	250 mL
Large egg	1	1
Unsweetened chocolate baking squares (1 oz., 28 g, each), melted	2	2
Sour cream	1 cup	250 mL
Vanilla	1 tsp.	5 mL
All-purpose flour	1¾ cups	425 mL
Baking powder	2 tsp.	10 mL
Baking soda	½ tsp.	2 mL
Salt	¼ tsp.	1 mL
Chopped walnuts	¾ cup	175 mL

Cream margarine, brown sugar and egg in large bowl. Mix in melted chocolate, sour cream and vanilla.

Add flour, baking powder, baking soda, salt and walnuts. Mix well. Drop by tablespoonfuls onto greased cookie sheet. Bake in 375°F (190°C) oven for 10 to 12 minutes. Makes about 5 dozen.

1 cookie: 66 Calories; 1 g Protein; 3.9 g Total Fat; 8 g Carbohydrate; 47 mg Sodium; trace Dietary Fiber

Pictured on page 75.

Peanut Butter Chippers

Chocolate and peanut butter flavors with a bit of a crunch from added peanuts.

Hard margarine, softened	½ cup	125 mL
Granulated sugar	¾ cup	175 mL
Brown sugar, packed	½ cup	125 mL
Smooth peanut butter	½ cup	125 mL
Large eggs	3	3
Vanilla	1 tsp.	5 mL
All-purpose flour	2 cups	500 mL
Cocoa, sifted	½ cup	125 mL
Baking powder	2 tsp.	10 mL
Salt	½ tsp.	2 mL
Chopped peanuts	⅓ cup	75 mL

Cream margarine and both sugars in large bowl. Mix in peanut butter. Beat in eggs, 1 at a time. Add vanilla. Mix.

Add remaining 5 ingredients. Stir well. Shape into 1¼ inch (3 cm) balls. Arrange on greased baking sheet. Press with floured fork. Bake in 400°F (205°C) oven for 8 to 9 minutes. Cookies will feel soft when hot. Makes 3½ dozen.

1 cookie: 101 Calories; 2 g Protein; 4.9 g Total Fat; 13 g Carbohydrate; 81 mg Sodium; 1 g Dietary Fiber

Pictured on page 75.

Truffle Gems

Not shaped like a truffle but the texture is truffle-like.

Semisweet chocolate chips	2 cups	500 mL
Cream cheese, softened and cut up	4 oz.	125 g
Large eggs	3	3
Granulated sugar	1 cup	250 mL
Vanilla	1½ tsp.	7 mL
All-purpose flour	1 cup	250 mL
Baking powder	¼ tsp.	1 mL
Icing (confectioner's) sugar	2 tbsp.	30 mL

Heat chocolate chips and cream cheese in medium saucepan over hot water, or on low, stirring constantly, until smooth. Do not overheat.

Beat eggs, sugar and vanilla in large bowl until light-colored and thickened. Add chocolate mixture. Beat until blended.

Add flour and baking powder. Mix well. Chill for 3 to 4 hours or overnight. Dough will be quite soft. Working with a portion of dough at a time, drop by rounded tablespoonfuls onto greased baking sheet. Bake in 350°F (175°C) oven for 10 to 12 minutes until set. Let stand for 5 minutes before removing to rack to cool.

Dust with icing sugar. Makes about 4 dozen.

1 cookie: 69 Calories; 1 g Protein; 3.4 g Total Fat; 10 g Carbohydrate; 12 mg Sodium; trace Dietary Fiber

Pictured on page 75.

1. Truffle Gems, above
2. Chocolate Cherry Cookies, page 76
3. Chocolate Chews, this page
4. Cookies From Cake, page 76
5. Peanut Butter Chippers, this page

Cookies From Cake

Cookies have a crackly look with a sugar coating.

Chocolate cake mix (2 layer size)	**1**	**1**
Frozen whipped topping, thawed	**4 cups**	**1 L**
Large egg, fork-beaten	**1**	**1**
Icing (confectioner's) sugar	**½ cup**	**125 mL**

Stir cake mix and whipped topping in large bowl. Mix in egg. Chill for several hours or overnight.

Drop by rounded tablespoonfuls into icing sugar. Carefully shape into round balls. Arrange on greased cookie sheet, allowing room for expansion. Bake in 375°F (190°C) oven for 10 to 12 minutes. Cool on pan for 1 minute before removing to rack. Makes 4 dozen.

1 cookie: 72 Calories; 1 g Protein; 2.9 g Total Fat; 11 g Carbohydrate; 62 mg Sodium; 0 g Dietary Fiber

Pictured on page 75.

Chocolate Shortbread

Handle with care. These are very fragile.

All-purpose flour	**1¾ cups**	**425 mL**
Brown sugar, packed	**⅓ cup**	**75 mL**
Cocoa, sifted	**¼ cup**	**60 mL**
Hard margarine, softened	**1 cup**	**250 mL**
Chopped pecans (or walnuts), optional		

Mix first 4 ingredients in large bowl. Shape into 2 logs, about 1½ inches (3.8 cm) in diameter each. Wrap in waxed paper. Chill for at least 1 hour. Cut into ¼ inch (6 mm) slices. Arrange on ungreased cookie sheet.

Press nut piece lightly into center of each cookie. Bake in 325°F (160°C) oven for 10 to 12 minutes. Makes 5 dozen cookies.

1 cookie: 49 Calories; 1 g Protein; 3.3 g Total Fat; 4 g Carbohydrate; 39 mg Sodium; trace Dietary Fiber

Pictured on page 77.

Chocolate Cherry Cookies

Such a winning tea cookie. A cherry center with a chocolate covering.

Hard margarine, softened	**⅔ cup**	**150 mL**
Granulated sugar	**1 cup**	**250 mL**
Large egg	**1**	**1**
Vanilla	**1 tsp.**	**5 mL**
All-purpose flour	**1½ cups**	**375 mL**
Cocoa, sifted	**⅓ cup**	**75 mL**
Baking soda	**½ tsp.**	**2 mL**
Salt	**¼ tsp.**	**1 mL**
Chopped pecans	**½ cup**	**125 mL**
Maraschino cherries, blotted dry with paper towel	**48**	**48**

Cream margarine and sugar in large bowl. Beat in egg and vanilla until creamy.

Work in flour, cocoa, baking soda and salt. Knead until very pliable.

Mix in pecans. Chill dough for 45 minutes.

Measure 1½ tsp. (7 mL) dough. Press flat and completely enclose 1 cherry. Repeat until all dough is used. Arrange balls on greased baking sheet. Bake in 350°F (175°C) oven for 10 to 12 minutes. Makes about 4 dozen.

1 cookie: 73 Calories; 1 g Protein; 3.8 g Total Fat; 10 g Carbohydrate; 62 mg Sodium; 1 g Dietary Fiber

Pictured on page 75.

Thumbprint Cookies

A fancy tea cookie that will always receive compliments.

Hard margarine, softened	3/4 cup	175 mL
Brown sugar, packed	1/2 cup	125 mL
Egg yolks (large)	2	2
All-purpose flour	1 1/4 cups	300 mL
Cocoa, sifted	1/4 cup	60 mL
Egg whites (large), fork-beaten	2	2
Finely chopped walnuts (or pecans)	1 1/2 cups	375 mL
Filling:		
Hard margarine	2 tbsp.	30 mL
White chocolate baking squares (1 oz., 28 g, each), cut up	4	4
Red jam (or jelly)	1/2 cup	125 mL

Cream margarine, brown sugar and egg yolks in large bowl.

Mix in flour and cocoa. Shape into 1 inch (2.5 cm) balls.

Dip each ball into egg white, then roll in walnuts. Arrange on greased baking sheet. Dent center of each with thumb. Bake in 350°F (175°C) oven for 5 minutes. Remove from oven. Press dents again. Bake for 8 to 10 minutes until golden brown.

Filling: Melt margarine and chocolate in small saucepan over hot water, or on low, stirring constantly, until smooth. Do not overheat. Spoon 1/2 tsp. (2 mL) chocolate into each dent. Top with 1/4 tsp. (1 mL) jam. Makes 3 dozen cookies.

1 cookie: 142 Calories; 2 g Protein; 9.5 g Total Fat; 13 g Carbohydrate; 64 mg Sodium; 1 g Dietary Fiber

Pictured on this page.

Left: Thumbprint Cookies, above
Right: Chocolate Shortbread, page 76

How do you prefer your chocolate?
Sweet and heady? Or subtle and smooth? These
recipes will help you make up your mind. This delightful selection
offers you the choice of whether to indulge fully in rich
chocolate, or to savor its tones in a more
modest, intriguing morsel.
A chocolate-lover's dream can come
true with Triple Chocolate Pizza. Cloud Meringue
offers a lighter flavor for appetites that have just enjoyed
a full course dinner. Remember, all good things
must come to an end—and when dessert
is the closing act on a spectacular meal, then
sing your finale in the key of c—chocolate!

Top: Ice-Cream Cake, page 82
(garnished with fresh strawberries and
grated chocolate, page 19)
Bottom: White Chocolate Orange Chill, page 82
(garnished with whipped topping, white chocolate curls,
page 20, orange peel strips and chocolate chips)

Ice-Cream Bombe

Takes a bit of extra time but the finished product is very picturesque.

Strawberry ice cream, slightly softened	**2 cups**	**500 mL**
Semisweet chocolate baking square (1 oz., 28 g), cut up	**½**	**½**
Chocolate ice cream, softened	**2 cups**	**500 mL**
Chocolate cake mix (1 layer size), prepared	**1**	**1**
Frozen light whipped topping, thawed	**2 cups**	**500 mL**
Semisweet chocolate chips, for garnish	**⅓ cup**	**75 mL**

Dampen inside of 1½ quart (1.5 L) bowl. Line with plastic wrap. Dampness helps to hold plastic in place. Press strawberry ice cream evenly in bottom and up sides. Freeze.

Melt chocolate in small saucepan on low, stirring often, until smooth. Tipping bowl, drizzle chocolate all over ice cream. Freeze.

Spoon chocolate ice cream into strawberry cavity.

Cut piece of cake to fit top of bowl. Place over ice cream. Freeze.

Turn out of bowl onto serving plate. Spread whipped topping over all. Melt chocolate in small bowl in microwave (30%). Drizzle over topping. Return to freezer or serve now. Cuts into 8 wedges.

1 wedge: 443 Calories; 6 g Protein; 27.7 g Total Fat; 45 g Carbohydrate; 247 mg Sodium; trace Dietary Fiber

Pictured on page 81.

Variation: For cake layer, use pound cake or brownies.

Baked Alaska

A showpiece for every dinner guest.

Slices of Chocolate Jelly Roll, page 40	**6**	**6**
Scoops of chocolate or strawberry ice cream	**6**	**6**
Meringue:		
Egg whites (large), room temperature	**2**	**2**
Cream of tartar	**¼ tsp.**	**1 mL**
Granulated sugar	**¼ cup**	**60 mL**

Arrange jelly roll slices on ungreased baking sheet. Place scoop of ice cream on each. Freeze.

Meringue: Beat egg whites and cream of tartar in small bowl until almost stiff. Add sugar gradually, while beating, until stiff and sugar is dissolved. Divide and spread over ice cream, covering completely to edge of jelly roll. Freeze. Bake in 450°F (230°C) oven for 3 to 4 minutes until lightly browned. Makes 6.

1 serving: 472 Calories; 7 g Protein; 21.7 g Total Fat; 65 g Carbohydrate; 241 mg Sodium; 2 g Dietary Fiber

Pictured on page 81.

Chocolate Fondue

Dip fresh fruit morsels in this almondy-rich fondue.

Semisweet chocolate baking squares (1 oz., 28 g, each), grated	**8**	**8**
Instant coffee granules, crushed to a powder	**2 tsp.**	**10 mL**
Whipping cream	**1 cup**	**250 mL**
Amaretto liqueur	**1 tbsp.**	**15 mL**

Mix chocolate and coffee powder in small bowl.

Heat ¾ cup (175 mL) whipping cream and liqueur in small saucepan on low, stirring constantly, just until warm. Add chocolate and coffee. Stir until chocolate is melted. To serve, pour remaining whipping cream into chocolate in thin swirl. Makes 1⅔ cups (400 mL).

⅓ cup (75 mL): 394 Calories; 3 g Protein; 32.2 g Total Fat; 29 g Carbohydrate; 25 mg Sodium; 3 g Dietary Fiber

Pictured on page 81.

Top Left: Chocolate Fondue, this page
Top Right and Bottom: Baked Alaska, this page
Center: Ice-Cream Bombe, this page

Ice-Cream Cake

A great budget-saver to make your own.

Hard margarine	**¾ cup**	**175 mL**
Chocolate wafer crumbs	**3 cups**	**750 mL**
Brown sugar, packed	**⅓ cup**	**75 mL**
Chocolate ice cream, softened	**8 cups**	**2 L**
Strawberry ice cream, softened	**8 cups**	**2 L**
Frozen light whipped topping, thawed	**2 cups**	**500 mL**

Melt margarine in medium saucepan. Stir in wafer crumbs and brown sugar. Divide into thirds. Press ⅓ of crumbs in bottom of ungreased 10 inch (25 cm) springform pan.

Spoon chocolate ice cream over crumb layer. Sprinkle with ⅓ of crumbs. Press lightly. Freeze.

Spoon strawberry ice cream over second crumb layer. Sprinkle with remaining crumbs. Press lightly. Freeze. Thaw for about 10 minutes. Run knife around pan to loosen sides.

Spread top only with whipped topping. Freeze. Cuts into 20 wedges.

1 wedge: 405 Calories; 5 g Protein; 24.4 g Total Fat; 44 g Carbohydrate; 255 mg Sodium; trace Dietary Fiber

Pictured on page 79.

Variation: Omit brown sugar. Add 2 crushed Skor, Heath or Crispy Crunch bars.

Variation: Drizzle your favorite sundae topping over one or both crumb layers.

White Chocolate Orange Chill

Orange flavor goes well with white chocolate.

Crust:		
Hard margarine	**⅓ cup**	**75 mL**
Chocolate wafer crumbs	**1½ cups**	**375 mL**
Filling:		
Frozen concentrated orange juice	**¼ cup**	**60 mL**
Prepared orange juice	**½ cup**	**125 mL**
Grand Marnier liqueur (or prepared orange juice)	**¼ cup**	**60 mL**
Lemon juice	**1 tsp.**	**5 mL**
Granulated sugar	**½ cup**	**125 mL**
Salt, just a pinch		
Envelope of unflavored gelatin	**¼ oz.**	**7 g**
Water	**¼ cup**	**60 mL**
Envelope of dessert topping (prepared according to package directions)	**1**	**1**
Grated white chocolate	**½ cup**	**125 mL**

Crust: Melt margarine in medium saucepan. Stir in wafer crumbs. Press in bottom and about 1 inch (2.5 cm) up side of ungreased 8 inch (20 cm) springform pan. Chill.

Filling: Stir first 6 ingredients in large bowl.

Sprinkle gelatin over water in small saucepan. Let stand for 1 minute. Heat and stir until dissolved. Stir into orange mixture. Cool slightly.

Fold dessert topping into orange mixture until no streaks of white can be seen. Gently fold in chocolate. Pour into springform pan. Chill. Cuts into 12 wedges.

1 wedge: 213 Calories; 2 g Protein; 10.3 g Total Fat; 27 g Carbohydrate; 131 mg Sodium; trace Dietary Fiber

Pictured on page 79.

Zuccotto

Delicious frozen or chilled. Makes a good impression.

Ingredient	Imperial	Metric
Cake:		
Large eggs	**2**	**2**
Granulated sugar	**¾ cup**	**175 mL**
Vanilla	**1 tsp.**	**5 mL**
All-purpose flour	**1 cup**	**250 mL**
Cocoa, sifted	**2 tbsp.**	**30 mL**
Baking powder	**1 tsp.**	**5 mL**
Salt	**¼ tsp.**	**1 mL**
Hard margarine	**1 tbsp.**	**15 mL**
Hot milk	**½ cup**	**125 mL**
Curaçao liqueur	**3 tbsp.**	**50 mL**
Kirsch liqueur	**3 tbsp.**	**50 mL**
Filling:		
Instant chocolate pudding powder, 4 serving size	**1**	**1**
Milk	**1 cup**	**250 mL**
Frozen light whipped topping, thawed	**4 cups**	**1 L**
Sliced hazelnuts (filberts), toasted and cooled	**½ cup**	**125 mL**
Semisweet chocolate baking squares (1 oz., 28 g, each), grated	**4**	**4**
Chocolate Glaze, page 23		

Cake: Beat eggs in large bowl until smooth. Beat in sugar and vanilla until light-colored and thickened. Stir in flour, cocoa, baking powder and salt.

Melt margarine in hot milk in small saucepan. Add to batter. Beat until smooth. Divide evenly into 2 round greased 9 inch (22 cm) layer cake pans. Bake in 350°F (175°C) oven for about 12 minutes. A wooden pick inserted in center should come out clean. Cool. Line dampened 8 cup (2 L) rounded dome-shaped bowl with plastic wrap. Ease 1 layer cake inside bowl. Push down to form shell. If cake breaks, fit in bowl as best you can.

Mix both liqueurs in small cup. Drizzle over cake in bowl.

Filling: Beat chocolate pudding powder and milk in large bowl until smooth.

Fold in whipped topping. Fold in hazelnuts and grated chocolate. Turn into cake-lined bowl. Trim remaining cake layer to fit over cream mixture, edge to edge. Freeze for at least 4 to 5 hours.

Turn cake out of bowl onto wire rack set on waxed paper. Pour glaze over Zuccotto to create smooth, even coating. Garnish as desired. Serve frozen for best results. Cuts into 12 wedges.

1 wedge: 447 Calories; 6 g Protein; 22.5 g Total Fat; 56 g Carbohydrate; 263 mg Sodium; 3 g Dietary Fiber

Pictured on front cover, page 9 and page 84/85.

Note: Garnish simply with white chocolate drizzle, page 22, or shaved white chocolate, page 19. Add more garnishings for a very spectacular look.

Chocolate Charlotte Russe

A scalloped edge of ladyfingers encloses this smooth, light dessert. For an added chocolate touch, dip one end of ladyfingers in melted chocolate.

Envelopes of unflavored gelatin (1/4 oz., 7 g, each)	2	2
Milk	2 1/2 cups	625 mL
Granulated sugar	2/3 cup	150 mL
Cocoa, sifted	1/2 cup	125 mL
Salt	1/4 tsp.	1 mL
Egg yolks (large)	3	3
Milk	2 tbsp.	30 mL
Vanilla	1 tsp.	5 mL
Egg whites (large), room temperature	3	3
Granulated sugar	1/3 cup	75 mL
Frozen whipped topping, thawed	2 cups	500 mL
Ladyfingers	30	30

Sprinkle gelatin over first amount of milk in medium saucepan. Let stand for 1 minute. Heat and stir until gelatin is dissolved. Bring mixture to a boil. Cool slightly.

Stir first amount of sugar, cocoa and salt in small bowl. Add egg yolks, second amount of milk and vanilla. Stir into boiling milk until just thickened. Set saucepan in ice water. Stir mixture frequently as it cools. Chill, stirring and scraping down sides often, until mixture will mound slightly. This thickens quickly.

Beat egg whites in medium bowl until soft peaks form. Gradually beat in second amount of sugar until stiff. Fold into gelatin mixture. Fold in whipped topping.

Cut 1 inch (2.5 cm) off 1 end of each ladyfinger. Stand enough ladyfingers, rounded or sugared side out and cut end down, around inside edge of greased 10 inch (25 cm) springform pan. Lay remaining ladyfingers and pieces in bottom of pan in single layer, breaking to fit. Spoon filling into pan, keeping ladyfingers from falling over. Chill. Cuts into 10 wedges.

1 wedge:267 Calories; 8 g Protein; 8.1 g Total Fat; 44 g Carbohydrate; 140 mg Sodium; 2 g Dietary Fiber

Pictured on page 87.

Marjolaine

This is a masterpiece!

Frozen puff pastry (14.1 oz., 397 g), thawed	1/2	1/2
Finely chopped hazelnuts (or almonds)	1/4 cup	60 mL
Filling:		
Light cream cheese, softened	4 oz.	125 g
Brown sugar, packed	1/2 cup	125 mL
Cold prepared strong coffee (or water)	3 tbsp.	50 mL
Semisweet chocolate chips	1 cup	250 mL
Ground hazelnuts (filberts)	1/2 cup	125 mL
Ground almonds	1/2 cup	125 mL
Frozen light whipped topping, thawed	4 cups	1 L

Roll 1 sheet of pastry on lightly floured surface into 13 × 13 inch (33 × 33 cm) square. Trim to 12 × 12 inch (30 × 30 cm) square with sharp knife to make straight edges. Cut into 3 equal strips forming 3 rectangles, 4 x 12 inch (10 x 30 cm) size. Poke surface of each several times with fork through to bottom. Arrange on ungreased baking sheet. Sprinkle with hazelnuts. Bake in 450°F (230°C) oven for about 8 minutes until puffed and golden. Cool. If not equal in size, use gentle sawing motion to trim.

Filling: Beat cream cheese, brown sugar and coffee in medium bowl until smooth.

Melt chocolate chips in small saucepan over hot water, or on low, stirring constantly, until smooth. Do not overheat. Cool to room temperature. Beat into cheese mixture.

Fold in hazelnuts and almonds. Fold in topping. Stack into 3 layers, spreading or piping about 1 2/3 cups (400 mL) chocolate mixture on each layer. Chill. Use gentle sawing motion to cut into 10 slices.

1 slice: 365 Calories; 6 g Protein; 22.8 g Total Fat; 39 g Carbohydrate; 297 mg Sodium; 2 g Dietary Fiber

Pictured on page 87.

Top: Marjolaine, above (garnished with Fudge Icing, page 110, and chocolate filigrees, page 24)
Bottom: Chocolate Charlotte Russe, this page ("tied" with a pink ribbon)

Truffle Cake

Incredible dessert. Truly melts in your mouth. Makes a special occasion even more special.

Crust:		
Hard margarine, softened	**½ cup**	**125 mL**
All-purpose flour	**1 cup**	**250 mL**
Icing (confectioner's) sugar	**⅓ cup**	**75 mL**
Cocoa, sifted	**2 tbsp.**	**30 mL**
Filling:		
Semisweet chocolate baking squares (1 oz., 28 g, each), cut up	**16**	**16**
Hard margarine	**½ cup**	**125 mL**
Vanilla	**1 tsp.**	**5 mL**
Egg yolks (large)	**4**	**4**
Egg whites (large), room temperature	**4**	**4**
Chocolate Glaze, page 23		

Crust: Mix all 4 ingredients in small bowl until mealy. Press in bottom of 8 inch (20 cm) springform pan. Set on piece of foil. Fold foil up outside of pan to prevent water leaking into pan. Set pan in larger pan or roaster.

Filling: Combine chocolate, margarine and vanilla in large saucepan. Heat over hot water, or on low, stirring constantly, until chocolate is melted and smooth. Do not overheat. Remove from heat.

Beat in egg yolks, 1 at a time.

Using clean beaters, beat egg whites in medium bowl until stiff. Fold into chocolate mixture. Pour over crust. Pour boiling water about ½ way up outside of pan. Bake in 425°F (220°C) oven for 15 minutes. Outer edge will be set. Center will be soft and look uncooked. Cool. Chill for several hours.

Remove sides of pan. Place cake on wire rack set on waxed paper. Pour glaze over cake, covering top and sides. Chill. Cuts into 16 wedges.

1 wedge: 401 Calories; 5 g Protein; 31.2 g Total Fat; 32 g Carbohydrate; 169 mg Sodium; 3 g Dietary Fiber

Pictured on page 90.

Chocolate Pâté

Most impressive. Can be prepared two days ahead. Do not freeze.

Butter (not margarine)	**1 cup**	**250 mL**
Semisweet chocolate chips	**3 cups**	**750 mL**
Instant coffee granules, crushed to a powder (optional)	**1 tsp.**	**5 mL**
Granulated sugar	**½ cup**	**125 mL**
Large eggs	**2**	**2**
Vanilla	**1 tsp.**	**5 mL**
Whipping cream	**1½ cups**	**375 mL**
Raspberry Coulis, page 153		
White chocolate baking squares (1 oz., 28 g, each), melted	**2**	**2**

Line 9 × 5 × 3 inch (22 × 12.5 × 7.5 cm) dampened loaf pan with plastic wrap. Melt butter in large saucepan over hot water, or on low. Add chocolate chips and coffee granules, stirring constantly, until smooth. Do not overheat. Pour into large bowl.

Add sugar. Beat well. Beat in eggs, 1 at a time. Beat until sugar is dissolved. Mix in vanilla.

Beat whipping cream in small bowl until stiff. Fold into chocolate mixture. Turn into pan. Cover loosely. Chill for at least 8 hours or overnight.

Unmold pâté onto platter. Cut slices ¾ inch (2 cm) thick with hot knife. Lay slice cut side down on individual plate. Spoon coulis on one side or all around slice. Make Heart Design, page 22, using melted white chocolate. Cuts into 16 slices.

1 slice: 493 Calories; 4 g Protein; 37.7 g Total Fat; 41 g Carbohydrate; 177 mg Sodium; 4 g Dietary Fiber

Pictured on page 91.

Backwards Fondue

The chocolate is in the dippers, not the fondue. Surround fondue with cubed chocolate pound cake, chocolate doughnuts, chocolate loaf cake, and chocolate fruit cake.

Fondue:

Can of sweetened condensed milk (or 14 oz., 398 mL, size)	**11 oz.**	**300 mL**
Dark corn syrup	**3/4 cup**	**175 mL**
Brown sugar, packed	**2 cups**	**500 mL**
Water	**2 tbsp.**	**30 mL**
Vanilla	**1 tsp.**	**5 mL**
Hard margarine	**1/4 cup**	**60 mL**

Fondue: Combine all 6 ingredients in heavy bottomed medium saucepan. Heat on low for about 8 minutes, stirring constantly, until thickened. Pour sauce into fondue pot. Keep warm over very low flame. Makes 2 3/4 cups (675 mL) sauce.

2 tbsp. (30 mL): 183 Calories; 1 g Protein; 3.6 g Total Fat; 37 g Carbohydrate; 61 mg Sodium; trace Dietary Fiber

Pictured on this page.

Top Left: Truffle Cake, page 88 (garnished with a crown of chocolate curls, page 20, and edged with Fudge Icing, page 110)
Top Right and Bottom: Chocolate Pâté, page 88

Deadly Chocolate Trifle

Serves a crowd unless real chocolate lovers get started at it. Brownies may be prepared hours ahead of time with Kahlúa if desired.

Fudge brownie mix (or your own), prepared	**1**	**1**
Kahlúa liqueur (or sweetened black coffee)	**1/3 cup**	**75 mL**
Instant chocolate mousse dessert mix (3.1 oz., 87 g, each), prepared	**3**	**3**
Chocolate-covered crispy toffee bars (such as Heath or Skor), 1 1/2 oz., 39 g, each, crushed (about 1 1/3 cups, 325 mL)	**8**	**8**
Frozen light whipped topping, thawed	**4 cups**	**1 L**

Make holes, using a fork, all over top of brownies. Drizzle Kahlúa over top. Let stand for 10 minutes. Chop brownies into small pieces. Divide into 2 piles. Put 1 pile into glass trifle bowl.

Layer 1/2 of mousse, 1/2 of crushed candy bars and 1/2 of whipped topping over brownies in bowl. Repeat layers, beginning with remaining pile of chopped brownies. Chill. Serves 20.

1 serving: 533 Calories; 7 g Protein; 31.1 g Total Fat; 59 g Carbohydrate; 154 mg Sodium; 1 g Dietary Fiber

Pictured on page 93.

Truffle Trifle

Wonderful for a crowd. Very easy to make half for a smaller group. Also known as Death By Chocolate. Best eaten fresh.

Chocolate cake mix (2 layer size)	**1**	**1**
Kahlúa liqueur (or 1/2 cup, 125 mL, cold coffee)	**2/3 cup**	**150 mL**
Instant chocolate pudding powders, 4 serving size each	**2**	**2**
Milk	**4 cups**	**1 L**
Frozen light whipped topping, thawed	**4 cups**	**1 L**
Chocolate-covered crispy toffee bars (such as Heath or Skor), 1 1/2 oz., 39 g, each, crushed (about 1 cup, 250 mL)	**6**	**6**

Prepare cake according to package directions. Bake in 2 greased 8 inch (20 cm) round layer cake pans. Cool. Remove 1 layer to cutting board, rounded side down.

Drizzle with 1/3 cup (75 mL) Kahlúa. Cut in 1 inch (2.5 cm) squares. Transfer to 6 quart (6 L) glass trifle bowl. Remove second cake layer from pan. Drizzle with remaining Kahlúa. Cut in 1 inch (2.5 cm) squares. Set aside.

Beat pudding powders and milk until smooth but not thickened. Pour 1/2 of pudding over cake in bowl.

Spread with 1/2 of whipped topping. Sprinkle 1/2 of crushed toffee bars over topping. Repeat layers, beginning with reserved cake pieces. Chill. Serves 20.

1 serving: 328 Calories; 4 g Protein; 11.3 g Total Fat; 50 g Carbohydrate; 393 mg Sodium; trace Dietary Fiber

Pictured on page 93.

Top: Deadly Chocolate Trifle, this page
(garnished with whipped topping)
Bottom: Truffle Trifle, above
(garnished with chocolate curls, page 20)

Velvet Lush

A cakey bottom layer with a wicked chocolate topping.

Chocolate Cake Crust:		
Hard margarine, softened	3 tbsp.	50 mL
Granulated sugar	1/3 cup	75 mL
All-purpose flour	1/4 cup	60 mL
Cocoa, sifted	2 tbsp.	30 mL
Large egg	1	1
Vanilla	1/4 tsp.	1 mL

Filling:		
Semisweet chocolate chips	3 cups	750 mL
Instant coffee granules, crushed to a powder	2 tsp.	10 mL
Hard margarine	1/4 cup	60 mL
Hot water	3/4 cup	175 mL
Rum flavoring	1 tsp.	5 mL
Brandy flavoring	1 tsp.	5 mL
Large eggs	2	2
Icing (confectioner's) sugar	1/4 cup	60 mL
Whipping cream (or 4 cups, 1 L, whipped topping)	2 cups	500 mL
Chocolate Glaze, page 23 (1/2 recipe)		

Chocolate Cake Crust: Measure all 6 ingredients into small bowl. Beat with spoon until smooth. Spread in greased 9 inch (22 cm) springform pan. Bake in 350°F (175°C) oven for about 10 minutes. A wooden pick inserted in center should come out clean. Cool.

Filling: Measure first 6 ingredients into saucepan. Heat on medium-low, stirring often, until smooth.

Beat in eggs, 1 at a time. Beat in icing sugar. Cool completely.

Beat whipping cream in bowl until stiff. Fold into chocolate mixture. Pour over cooled crust. Chill for at least 2 hours.

Remove sides of pan. Place cake on wire rack set on waxed paper. Pour glaze over top of cake, letting some run down sides. Cuts into 12 wedges.

1 wedge: 500 Calories; 5 g Protein; 40 g Total Fat; 38 g Carbohydrate; 123 mg Sodium; 3 g Dietary Fiber

Pictured on page 95.

Velvet Lush, page 94 (garnished with sliced Prickly Pear and chocolate-covered coffee beans)

Chocolate Angel Dessert

A yummy mousse-like dessert. Has a unique look.

Envelope of unflavored gelatin	**¼ oz.**	**7 g**
Water	**½ cup**	**125 mL**
Semisweet chocolate chips	**1 cup**	**250 mL**
Egg yolks (large), fork-beaten	**4**	**4**
Egg whites (large), room temperature	**4**	**4**
Envelope of dessert topping (not prepared)	**1**	**1**
Milk	**½ cup**	**125 mL**
Chopped pecans (or almonds), optional	**⅓ cup**	**75 mL**
Large angel food cake, cut into slices then into cubes	**1**	**1**
Chopped pecans (or almonds), for garnish	**⅓ cup**	**75 mL**

Sprinkle gelatin over water in small saucepan. Let stand for 1 minute. Heat, stirring constantly, until dissolved.

Add chocolate chips. Heat and stir on low until melted. Slowly stir in beaten yolks. Pour into large bowl. Cool to lukewarm.

Beat egg whites in medium bowl until stiff. Fold into chocolate mixture.

Beat topping mix and milk in small bowl until stiff. Fold into chocolate mixture.

Add first amount of pecans. Fold in.

Scatter ½ of cake chunks in ungreased 9 × 13 inch (22 × 33 cm) pan. Spoon ½ of chocolate mixture over top. Repeat both layers.

Sprinkle with second amount of pecans. Chill for several hours. Cuts into 15 pieces.

1 piece: 201 Calories; 5 g Protein; 6.2 g Total Fat; 33 g Carbohydrate; 88 mg Sodium; 1 g Dietary Fiber

Pictured on page 97.

Strawberry Sundae Cake

Family and guests are lucky when this is in the freezer.

Dark chocolate cake mix (2 layer size)	**1**	**1**
Instant vanilla pudding powder, 4 serving size	**1**	**1**
Cooking oil	**½ cup**	**125 mL**
Large eggs	**4**	**4**
Water	**1 cup**	**250 mL**
Strawberry ice cream	**2 qts.**	**2 L**
Hot Fudge Sauce, page 153, heated		
Toasted pecans, chopped	**2 tbsp.**	**30 mL**
Maraschino cherries, with stems, drained	**15**	**15**

Place first 5 ingredients in large bowl. Beat on low until moistened. Beat on medium for about 2 minutes until smooth. Turn into greased 9 × 13 inch (22 × 33 cm) pan. Bake in 350°F (175°C) oven for about 35 minutes. A wooden pick inserted in center should come out clean. Cool. Remove from pan. Cut in half horizontally to make 2 layers. Return bottom layer to pan.

Slice ice cream into layers. Cover bottom layer of cake using all of ice cream. Set second layer of cake on top. Cover. Freeze.

To serve, cut and place piece on individual plate. Spoon on about 2 tbsp. (30 mL) sauce per serving, sprinkle with pecans and top with cherry. Cuts into 15 pieces.

1 piece: 548 Calories; 7 g Protein; 25.7 g Total Fat; 76 g Carbohydrate; 329 mg Sodium; 1 g Dietary Fiber

Pictured on page 97.

Vanilla Sundae Cake

Use vanilla ice cream rather than strawberry.

Top: Chocolate Angel Dessert, this page
Bottom: Strawberry Sundae Cake, above

Semifreddo

This say-mee-FRAYD-doh is an eye-catching dark and light dessert.

Envelopes of unflavored gelatin (1/4 oz., 7 g, each)	**3**	**3**
Water	**3/4 cup**	**175 mL**
Light cream cheese, softened	**8 oz.**	**250 g**
Granulated sugar	**1 cup**	**250 mL**
Non-fat sour cream	**2 cups**	**500 mL**
Instant vanilla pudding powder, 4 serving size	**1**	**1**
Milk	**1 cup**	**250 mL**
Frozen light whipped topping, thawed	**1 cup**	**250 mL**
Chocolate Mixture:		
Hard margarine	**1/2 cup**	**125 mL**
Chocolate wafer crumbs	**2 cups**	**500 mL**
Brown sugar, packed	**2 tbsp.**	**30 mL**
Finely chopped pecans (or walnuts)	**1/2 cup**	**125 mL**

Sprinkle gelatin over water in medium saucepan. Let stand for 1 minute. Heat, stirring constantly, until dissolved. Cool.

Beat cream cheese and sugar in large bowl until smooth. Beat in gelatin mixture.

Add next 3 ingredients. Beat well.

Fold in whipped topping.

Chocolate Mixture: Melt margarine in medium saucepan. Stir in chocolate crumbs, brown sugar and pecans. Pack 1/3 of chocolate mixture in foil-lined 9 × 5 × 3 inch (22 × 12 × 7.5 cm) loaf pan. Pour 1/2 of cheese mixture over top. Chill mixture in loaf pan until fairly firm. Sprinkle with 1/3 chocolate mixture. Press lightly. Pour remaining cheese mixture over top. Sprinkle with remaining 1/3 chocolate mixture. Press lightly. Chill overnight. Cuts into 12 slices.

1 slice: 397 Calories; 7 g Protein; 21.4 g Total Fat; 48 g Carbohydrate; 430 mg Sodium; 1 g Dietary Fiber

Pictured on page 98/99.

Semifreddo, above (drizzled with Raspberry Coulis, page 153, and garnished with whipped topping and raspberries)

Pudding Ice Cream

Not only good ice cream but can be frozen in fudgsicle forms.

Granulated sugar	1 cup	250 mL
Chocolate pudding powder (not instant), 6 serving size	1	1
Cocoa, sifted	1/4 cup	60 mL
Milk	3 cups	750 mL
Can of evaporated milk	13 1/2 oz.	385 mL
Vanilla	1 tbsp.	15 mL

Stir sugar, pudding powder and cocoa in large saucepan. Stir in first amount of milk. Heat, stirring often, until mixture comes to a rolling boil that cannot be stirred down. Remove from heat. Set saucepan in cold water in sink. Stir. Lay plastic wrap or waxed paper directly on pudding to stop crust from forming. Cool.

Add evaporated milk and vanilla. Stir well. Chill until very cold. Turn into 2 quart (2 L) ice-cream maker. Freeze according to directions. Makes 6 cups (1.5 L) ice cream.

1/2 cup (125 mL): 180 Calories; 6 g Protein; 1.2 g Total Fat; 39 g Carbohydrate; 136 mg Sodium; 2 g Dietary Fiber

Pictured on page 102.

Easy Chocolate Ice Cream

Nice smooth texture.

Chocolate milk	3 cups	750 mL
Can of sweetened condensed milk (or 14 oz., 398 mL)	11 oz.	300 mL
Frozen whipped topping, thawed	1 1/2 cups	375 mL

Whisk both milks in large bowl until smooth. Add whipped topping. Stir well. Pour into 2 quart (2 L) ice-cream maker. Freeze according to directions. Makes 6 cups (1.5 L) ice cream.

1/2 cup (125 mL): 182 Calories; 5 g Protein; 6.6 g Total Fat; 27 g Carbohydrate; 83 mg Sodium; trace Dietary Fiber

Pictured on page 103.

White Chocolate Ice Cream

A rich, smooth velvet texture.

Milk	2 cups	500 mL
Granulated sugar	3/4 cup	175 mL
All-purpose flour	1 tbsp.	15 mL
Salt	1/2 tsp.	2 mL
Large egg	1	1
White chocolate baking squares (1 oz., 28 g, each), cut up	6	6
Vanilla	1/2 tsp.	2 mL
Whipping cream	2 cups	500 mL

Pour milk into top of double boiler. Heat over boiling water until very hot.

Combine sugar, flour and salt in small bowl. Beat in egg until smooth. Stir into hot milk. Heat, stirring constantly, for 3 minutes. Remove from heat.

Add chocolate. Stir until melted. Chill for several hours or overnight.

Stir in vanilla and whipping cream. Pour into 2 quart (2 L) ice-cream maker. Freeze according to directions. Makes 6 cups (1.5 L) ice cream.

1/2 cup (125 mL): 285 Calories; 4 g Protein; 18.9 g Total Fat; 26 g Carbohydrate; 168 mg Sodium; trace Dietary Fiber

Pictured on page 103.

Mocha Mousse

Simple and quick. Bowls of froth.

Strong coffee	**1 cup**	**250 mL**
Large marshmallows	**30**	**30**
Semisweet chocolate chips	**1½ cups**	**375 mL**
Envelope of dessert topping (not prepared)	**1**	**1**
Milk	**½ cup**	**125 mL**

Heat coffee and marshmallows in large saucepan, stirring occasionally, until marshmallows are melted.

Add chocolate chips. Stir until melted. Cool thoroughly.

Beat dessert topping mix and milk in small bowl until stiff. Fold into chocolate mixture. Divide among serving dishes. Makes 4 cups (1 L).

½ cup (125 mL): 266 Calories; 3 g Protein; 12.2 g Total Fat; 41 g Carbohydrate; 43 mg Sodium; 2 g Dietary Fiber

Pictured on this page.

Triple Chocolate Pizza

The photo says it all!

Chocolate Pizza Crust:		
All-purpose flour	2 cups	500 mL
Granulated sugar	1¼ cups	300 mL
Cocoa, sifted	⅓ cup	75 mL
Hard margarine, softened	¾ cup	175 mL
Large eggs, fork-beaten	2	2
Chocolate Filling:		
Cream cheese, softened	8 oz.	250 g
Granulated sugar	¾ cup	175 mL
Large egg	1	1
Cocoa, sifted	¼ cup	60 mL
Vanilla	1 tsp.	5 mL
Topping:		
Semisweet chocolate chips	⅓ cup	75 mL
White chocolate chips	⅓ cup	75 mL
Butterscotch chips	⅓ cup	75 mL
Maraschino cherries, drained and halved	8-10	8-10
Sliced almonds	1-2 tbsp.	15-30 mL

Chocolate Pizza Crust: Measure flour, sugar and cocoa into bowl. Add margarine. Cut in until crumbly.

Add eggs. Mix well. Press in greased 12 inch (30 cm) pizza pan. Bake in 350°F (175°C) oven for 15 minutes.

Chocolate Filling: Beat all 5 ingredients together until smooth. Spread over hot crust. Return to oven for 10 minutes.

Topping: Sprinkle with 3 kinds of chips. Let stand until soft. Draw tip of knife back and forth over top to smooth out most of the chips. If necessary, return to warm oven for a minute.

Place cherries here and there. Place almond slices around edge. Cool. Cuts into 12 wedges.

1 wedge: 493 Calories; 7 g Protein; 24.5 g Total Fat; 65 g Carbohydrate; 229 mg Sodium; 3 g Dietary Fiber

Pictured on page 102/103.

Top: Triple Chocolate Pizza, above
Left: Pudding Ice Cream, page 100
Bottom Center: White Chocolate Ice Cream, page 100
Bottom Right: Easy Chocolate Ice Cream, page 100

Cloud Meringue

An extra-special dessert.
Make in the morning or the day before.
Cut with a warm, damp knife.

Meringues:		
Egg whites (large), room temperature	**4**	**4**
Cream of tartar	**¼ tsp.**	**1 mL**
Granulated sugar	**1 cup**	**250 mL**
Cocoa, sifted	**1 tbsp.**	**15 mL**
Filling:		
Semisweet chocolate chips	**1 cup**	**250 mL**
Water	**3 tbsp.**	**50 mL**
Envelopes of dessert topping (not prepared)	**2**	**2**
Milk	**1 cup**	**250 mL**
Cocoa, sifted	**2 tsp.**	**10 mL**
Skor (or Heath) candy bars (1½ oz., 39 g, each), coarsely crushed	**6**	**6**

Meringues: Draw 2 circles, 8 inches (20 cm) in diameter, on lightly greased foil on baking sheet. Beat egg whites and cream of tartar in large bowl until soft peaks form.

Gradually add sugar, beating until stiff and glossy. Sift cocoa over top. Fold in. Spread ½ of egg whites in each circle. Bake in 250°F (120°C) oven for 1 hour. Turn off heat. Let meringues stand in oven for 1 hour before removing to cool completely.

Filling: Heat chocolate chips and water in small saucepan over hot water, or on low, stirring constantly, until smooth. Do not overheat. Loosen meringues from foil. Spread ½ of chocolate mixture on each to edge.

Beat next 3 ingredients in small bowl until stiff.

Fold in crushed candy bars. Spread ½ of filling over each chocolate-covered meringue. Carefully lift 1 meringue and place on top of other meringue. Chill for 8 hours before serving. Cuts into 12 wedges.

1 wedge: 263 Calories; 4 g Protein; 9.5 g Total Fat; 44 g Carbohydrate; 97 mg Sodium; 1 g Dietary Fiber

Pictured on page 105.

Chocolate Torte

Nuts replace the flour in this incredible indulgence.

Hard margarine, softened	**½ cup**	**125 mL**
Egg yolks (large)	**5**	**5**
Cocoa, sifted	**2 tbsp.**	**30 mL**
Semisweet chocolate chips	**1 cup**	**250 mL**
Egg whites (large), room temperature	**5**	**5**
Granulated sugar	**½ cup**	**125 mL**
Pecans (or walnuts or almonds), ground	**1¼ cups**	**300 mL**
Cocoa Glaze, page 23		

Cream margarine well in medium bowl. Add egg yolks, 1 at a time, beating well after each addition. Beat in cocoa.

Melt chocolate chips in small saucepan over hot water, or on low, stirring constantly, until smooth. Do not overheat. Beat into egg mixture.

Using clean beaters, beat egg whites in large bowl until soft peaks form. Gradually add sugar, beating until stiff. Fold ¼ of whites into chocolate mixture. Fold in remaining whites.

Add pecans. Fold in. Pour into greased and floured 9 inch (22 cm) springform pan. Bake in 350°F (175°C) oven for 35 to 40 minutes. A wooden pick inserted in center should come out clean. Place pan on rack. Run knife around edge to loosen. Cool completely.

Remove sides of pan. Place torte on wire rack set on waxed paper. Pour glaze over top and down sides of torte. Cuts into 12 wedges.

1 wedge: 357 Calories; 5 g Protein; 28.6 g Total Fat; 26 g Carbohydrate; 128 mg Sodium; 3 g Dietary Fiber

Pictured on page 105.

Top: Cloud Meringue, this page (garnished with pieces of fresh fruit)
Bottom: Chocolate Torte, above (garnished with chocolate chips)

Dacquoise

Pronounced da-KWAHZ. Garnish with chocolate curls, whipped topping and fresh strawberries for a touch of color.

Meringue Layers:		
Egg whites (large), room temperature	**6**	**6**
Cream of tartar	**½ tsp.**	**2 mL**
Granulated sugar	**1½ cups**	**375 mL**
Ground almonds	**⅓ cup**	**75 mL**
Ground hazelnuts	**⅓ cup**	**75 mL**
Cocoa, sifted	**3 tbsp.**	**50 mL**
Cornstarch	**1 tbsp.**	**15 mL**
Filling:		
Milk	**1½ cups**	**375 mL**
Chocolate pudding powder (not instant), 6 serving size	**1**	**1**
Light cream cheese, softened	**8 oz.**	**250 g**
Granulated sugar	**½ cup**	**125 mL**
Milk	**⅓ cup**	**75 mL**

Line 2 baking sheets with foil. Draw 2 circles, 9 inches (22 cm) in diameter, on foil.

Meringue Layers: Beat egg whites and cream of tartar in large bowl until soft peak stage. Gradually add sugar, beating until very stiff.

Fold in almonds and hazelnuts. Sift cocoa and cornstarch over top. Fold in. Spread ½ of mixture on each circle to traced edges. Smooth tops and sides. Bake in 250°F (120°C) oven for 1 hour. Turn off heat. Let stand in oven for 1 hour before removing to cool completely.

Filling: Heat first amount of milk in medium saucepan until boiling.

Beat remaining 4 ingredients in medium bowl until smooth. Stir into milk until boiling and thickened. Set saucepan in cold water to cool completely, stirring mixture often. Spread ½ on each layer. Stack layers on serving plate. Chill. Cuts into 12 wedges.

1 wedge: 289 Calories; 7 g Protein; 7.1 g Total Fat; 53 g Carbohydrate; 325 mg Sodium; 2 g Dietary Fiber

Pictured on page 107.

Eclairs In A Pan

A bit of a twist on the real thing. Pastry-like with a rich filling. Fabulous.

Whole graham crackers (14½ oz., 400 g)	**60**	**60**
Instant chocolate pudding pudding powder, 4 serving size	**1**	**1**
Milk	**1½ cups**	**375 mL**
Frozen whipped topping, thawed	**1 cup**	**250 mL**
Instant pistachio (or vanilla) pudding powder, 4 serving size	**1**	**1**
Milk	**1½ cups**	**375 mL**
Frozen whipped topping, thawed	**1 cup**	**250 mL**
Smooth Chocolate Icing, page 109		

Arrange ⅓ of graham crackers in 9 × 13 inch (22 × 33 cm) pan to cover bottom.

Beat chocolate pudding powder and first amount of milk in medium bowl for 2 minutes. Fold first amount of topping into pudding. Spread over graham crackers in pan. Cover with another layer of crackers.

Beat pistachio pudding mix and second amount of milk in medium bowl for 2 minutes. Fold second amount of topping into pudding. Spread over graham crackers in pan. Cover with layer of remaining crackers.

Spread icing over top layer of crackers. Chill for at least 8 hours or overnight. Cuts into 16 pieces.

1 piece: 300 Calories; 4 g Protein; 8.1 g Total Fat; 57 g Carbohydrate; 288 mg Sodium; 1 g Dietary Fiber

Pictured on page 107.

Top: Dacquoise, this page
Bottom: Eclairs In A Pan, above

It's a virtual cornucopia of treats—even the sweetest of dreams was never this delicious! Of course there is the classic and perennial favorite Chocolate Icing, but you'll also find some creative alternatives to sample—delicately flavored icings to complement any cake and lavish fillings that simply burst with flavor. Keep your eye on the mixing bowl though—a few stray fingers may wander in for a quick sample when you turn your back!

Icings, Fillings & Frostings

Smooth Chocolate Icing

Rich chocolate flavor. Do not freeze. Use for Eclairs In A Pan, page 106.

Granulated sugar	1 cup	250 mL
Cornstarch	1/4 cup	60 mL
Salt	1/4 tsp.	1 mL
Hot water	1 cup	250 mL
Unsweetened chocolate baking squares (1 oz., 28 g, each), cut up	2	2
Hard margarine	1 tbsp.	15 mL
Icing (confectioner's) sugar	1/2 cup	125 mL

Stir sugar, cornstarch and salt in medium saucepan. Add water. Stir. Heat, stirring constantly, until boiling and thickened.

Add chocolate and margarine, stirring constantly, until melted and smooth. Set saucepan in cold water, stirring mixture often, until cool.

Stir in icing sugar, adding more or less to make proper spreading consistency. Makes 1 2/3 cups (400 mL).

1 tbsp. (15 mL): 57 Calories; trace Protein; 1.6 g Total Fat; 11 g Carbohydrate; 30 mg Sodium; trace Dietary Fiber

Pictured on page 107.

Chocolate Whipped Topping

A light brown fluffy topping. Not too sweet. Great for Pumpkin Chip Cake, page 38, and Chocolate Amaretto Cheesecake, page 66.

Semisweet chocolate chips	1 cup	250 mL
Envelopes of dessert topping (not prepared)	2	2
Milk	1 cup	250 mL
Vanilla	1 tsp.	5 mL

Melt chocolate chips in medium saucepan over hot water, or on low, stirring constantly, until smooth. Do not overheat. Cool to room temperature.

Beat topping mix, milk and vanilla in medium bowl until stiff. Add cooled chocolate. Beat to combine. Ice top and sides of 2 layer cake. Makes 5 cups (1.25 L).

1/4 cup (60 mL): 68 Calories; 1 g Protein; 4.5 g Total Fat; 7 g Carbohydrate; 13 mg Sodium; trace Dietary Fiber

Pictured on page 39.

Chocolate Butter Icing

A pale chocolate color. Rich like expensive commercial cakes. Use to fill Chocolate Jelly Roll, page 40.

Butter (not margarine), softened	3/4 cup	175 mL
Boiling water	1/4 cup	60 mL
Vanilla	1/2 tsp.	2 mL
Icing (confectioner's) sugar	2 cups	500 mL
Cocoa, sifted	1/4 cup	60 mL

Beat all 5 ingredients in medium bowl until mixture lightens in both color and texture. Makes generous 2 cups (500 mL).

1 tbsp. (15 mL): 68 Calories; 0 g Protein; 4.4 g Total Fat; 8 g Carbohydrate; 45 mg Sodium; trace Dietary Fiber

Pictured on page 40/41.

Fudge Icing

A quick, shiny, very tasty icing.

Semisweet chocolate chips	**1 cup**	**250 mL**
Sour cream	**1 cup**	**250 mL**

Heat chocolate chips and sour cream in medium saucepan over hot water, or on low, stirring constantly, until smooth. Cool to room temperature. Makes 1⅔ cups (400 mL).

½ tbsp. (7 mL): 40 Calories; 1 g Protein; 1.9 g Total Fat; 6 g Carbohydrate; 20 mg Sodium; trace Dietary Fiber

Pictured on pages 46, 49, 69, 91 and 137.

Chocolate Butter

Perfect for dressing up muffins or loaves.

Hard margarine, softened	**½ cup**	**125 mL**
Granulated sugar	**2 tbsp.**	**30 mL**
Cocoa, sifted	**2 tbsp.**	**30 mL**

Beat all 3 ingredients in small bowl until smooth. Makes ½ cup (125 mL).

2 tsp. (10 mL): 79 Calories; trace Protein; 7.9 g Total Fat; 3 g Carbohydrate; 92 mg Sodium; trace Dietary Fiber

Pictured on page 123.

Chocolate Icing

Use to ice Chocolate Pound Cake, page 42.
Double recipe to ice a layer cake.

Semisweet chocolate baking squares (1 oz., 28 g, each), cut up	**2**	**2**
Milk	**¼ cup**	**60 mL**
Hard margarine	**¼ cup**	**60 mL**
Vanilla	**1 tsp.**	**5 mL**
Icing (confectioner's) sugar	**3 cups**	**750 mL**

Place chocolate, milk, margarine and vanilla in medium saucepan. Heat on low, stirring constantly, until smooth. Remove from heat.

Mix in icing sugar, adding more milk or icing sugar if needed to make proper spreading consistency. Makes 1⅓ cups (325 mL).

1 tbsp. (15 mL): 98 Calories; trace Protein; 3.2 g Total Fat; 18 g Carbohydrate; 28 mg Sodium; trace Dietary Fiber

Pictured on page 43.

Mocha Fluff Icing

Good flavor without sweetness. Just right for a sweet cake.
Use for Chocolate Hazelnut Cake, page 44.

Envelope of dessert topping (not prepared)	**1**	**1**
Milk	**½ cup**	**125 mL**
Instant coffee granules, crushed to a powder	**1 tbsp.**	**15 mL**
Cocoa, sifted	**1 tbsp.**	**15 mL**

Combine topping mix, milk and coffee granules in small bowl. Beat on low to moisten. Beat on medium until stiff.

Add cocoa. Beat well. Makes 1½ cups (375 mL).

1 tbsp. (15 mL): 13 Calories; trace Protein; 0.8 g Total Fat; 1 g Carbohydrate; 5 mg Sodium; trace Dietary Fiber

Pictured on page 45.

Creamy Chocolate Frosting

Smooth and creamy. Firms when chilled. Use to ice Crusty Brownies, page 160.

Water	**⅓ cup**	**75 mL**
Granulated sugar	**⅓ cup**	**75 mL**
Egg yolks (large)	**3**	**3**
Semisweet chocolate baking squares (1 oz., 28 g, each), melted and cooled to room temperature	**5**	**5**
Hard margarine, softened	**⅓ cup**	**75 mL**

Stir water and sugar together in small saucepan until dissolved. Bring to a boil. Boil, without stirring, for 1 minute.

Beat egg yolks on high until thick. Gradually add hot syrup and chocolate while beating. Add margarine. Beat well until smooth. Chill until thickened to spreading consistency. Store iced product in fridge due to egg yolks. Makes 1⅓ cups (325 mL).

1 tbsp. (15 mL): 80 Calories; 1 g Protein; 6 g Total Fat; 7 g Carbohydrate; 37 mg Sodium; trace Dietary Fiber

Pictured on page 162/163.

Chocolate Cheese Icing

Light in color. Goes well with a dark chocolate cake, such as Chocolate Date Cake, page 38.

Unsweetened chocolate baking squares (1 oz., 28 g, each), cut up	**3**	**3**
Cream cheese, softened	**8 oz.**	**250 g**
Vanilla	**1 tsp.**	**5 mL**
Milk	**1 tbsp.**	**15 mL**
Icing (confectioner's) sugar	**4 cups**	**1 L**

Melt chocolate in small saucepan over hot water, or on low, stirring constantly, until smooth. Do not overheat. Remove from heat.

Beat cream cheese, vanilla, milk and about ⅓ of icing sugar in medium bowl. Add remaining icing sugar. Beat until smooth. Add chocolate. Beat to mix. Makes 2¾ cups (675 mL).

1 tbsp. (15 mL): 70 Calories; 1 g Protein; 2.9 g Total Fat; 11 g Carbohydrate; 17 mg Sodium; trace Dietary Fiber

Pictured on page 39.

Sour Cream Icing

Great on Chocolate Cake, page 48.

Semisweet chocolate chips	**1 cup**	**250 mL**
Hard margarine	**¼ cup**	**60 mL**
Sour cream	**½ cup**	**125 mL**
Vanilla	**1 tsp.**	**5 mL**
Icing (confectioner's) sugar	**4 cups**	**1 L**

Melt chocolate chips and margarine in large saucepan over hot water, or on low, stirring constantly, until smooth. Do not overheat. Remove from heat.

Add sour cream, vanilla and icing sugar. Beat on low to moisten. Beat on medium until fluffy. Add a bit more sour cream or icing sugar if needed for proper spreading consistency. Makes 2¾ cups (675 mL).

1 tbsp. (15 mL): 68 Calories; 0 g Protein; 2.6 g Total Fat; 12 g Carbohydrate; 14 mg Sodium; trace Dietary Fiber

Pictured on page 49.

White Chocolate Icing

Very nice flavor. Complements any cake, especially White Chocolate Pound Cake, page 44.

Hard margarine	**½ cup**	**125 mL**
White chocolate baking squares (1 oz., 28 g, each), cut up	**6**	**6**
Icing (confectioner's) sugar	**4 cups**	**1 L**
Vanilla	**1 tsp.**	**5 mL**
Milk	**2 tbsp.**	**30 mL**

Melt margarine and chocolate in medium saucepan over hot water, or on low, stirring constantly, until smooth. Do not overheat. Remove from heat.

Mix in icing sugar, vanilla and milk, adding more milk or icing sugar as needed for proper spreading consistency. Beat well. Makes 2⅔ cups (650 mL).

1 tbsp. (15 mL): 85 Calories; 0 g Protein; 3.4 g Total Fat; 13 g Carbohydrate; 30 mg Sodium; 0 g Dietary Fiber

Pictured on page 45.

Chocolate Spread

Spread on bread, tea loaves or muffins.

Cream cheese, softened	**4 oz.**	**125 g**
Milk	**1½ tbsp.**	**25 mL**
Icing (confectioner's) sugar	**¼ cup**	**60 mL**
Semisweet chocolate chips, melted	**¼ cup**	**60 mL**
Ground hazelnuts (filberts), toasted	**¼ cup**	**60 mL**
Vanilla	**½ tsp.**	**2 mL**

Combine all 6 ingredients in small bowl. Beat together well. Makes 1 cup (250 mL).

1 tbsp. (15 mL): 53 Calories; 1 g Protein; 4.2 g Total Fat; 4 g Carbohydrate; 23 mg Sodium; trace Dietary Fiber

Pictured on page 123.

Cassata Filling

Change a chocolate cake into an Italian-type cake—just spread filling between layers. Or use to fill Chocolate Cups, page 176.

Part-skim ricotta cheese	**8 oz.**	**250 g**
Granulated sugar	**2 tbsp.**	**30 mL**
Grated semisweet chocolate	**3 tbsp.**	**50 mL**
Cut glazed mixed fruit, chopped smaller yet (or chopped glazed cherries)	**3 tbsp.**	**50 mL**

Beat cheese and sugar in small bowl until texture is creamy.

Stir in chocolate and fruit. Makes 1½ cups (375 mL) filling.

1 tbsp. (15 mL): 27 Calories; 1 g Protein; 1.2 g Total Fat; 3 g Carbohydrate; 14 mg Sodium; trace Dietary Fiber

Pictured on page 178 and page 179.

Chocolate Caramel Filling

A good filling and topping for Jelly Roll Cake, page 48. Reserve about 2 tbsp. (30 mL) chopped candy bar for garnish, if desired.

Envelopes of dessert topping (not prepared)	**2**	**2**
Milk	**1 cup**	**250 mL**
Cocoa, sifted	**¼ cup**	**60 mL**
Icing (confectioner's) sugar	**¼ cup**	**60 mL**
Salt	**⅛ tsp.**	**0.5 mL**
Heath (or Skor) candy bars (1½ oz., 39 g, each), finely chopped	**3**	**3**

Beat topping mix and milk in medium bowl until stiff.

Add cocoa. Beat well. Beat in icing sugar and salt. Fold in chopped candy bar. Makes 5 cups (1.25 L).

4 tbsp. (60 mL): 59 Calories; 1 g Protein; 2.4 g Total Fat; 9 g Carbohydrate; 43 mg Sodium; 1 g Dietary Fiber

Pictured on page 49.

It may sound a little odd to add chocolate to a main course dish, but it's actually a common practice in a number of countries. After all, before sugar is added, chocolate has a rather bitter and distinctive flavor, like many other spices. Mole (pronounced MOH-lay) is the name given to a sauce made from chilies plus often a combination of chocolate and a wide variety of other ingredients such as vegetables, spices, sesame seeds and raisins. With this concoction, chicken can be marinated, turkey can be basted and almost any main dish flavor enhanced. This selection of recipes demonstrates the true versatility of chocolate and can inspire even the biggest skeptic of chocolate to sing its virtues.

Main Dishes

Chili Mole

A dark, rich color. More chili powder can be added if desired.

Lean ground beef	1 lb.	454 g
Chopped onion	1 cup	250 mL
Condensed tomato soup	10 oz.	284 mL
Can of kidney beans, with liquid	14 oz.	398 mL
Grated carrot	½ cup	125 mL
Water	1 cup	250 mL
Beef bouillon powder	1 tsp.	5 mL
Worcestershire sauce	1 tsp.	5 mL
Salt	½ tsp.	2 mL
Pepper	¼ tsp.	1 mL
Liquid smoke	¼ tsp.	1 mL
Chili powder	2 tsp.	10 mL
Cocoa, sifted	1 tbsp.	15 mL

Brown ground beef and onion in non-stick frying pan. Drain. Turn into large saucepan.

Add remaining 11 ingredients. Stir well. Bring to a boil. Simmer, covered, for about 15 minutes, stirring occasionally, until carrot is cooked. Serves 6.

1 serving: 228 Calories; 19 g Protein; 7.6 g Total Fat; 22 g Carbohydrate; 976 mg Sodium; 6 g Dietary Fiber

Pictured on this page.

Beans Mole

A rich, deep color and flavor. Serve as a tasty side dish for ribs, roast or other meats.

Chopped onion	**¼ cup**	**60 mL**
Hard margarine	**1 tsp.**	**5 mL**
Can of beans in tomato sauce	**14 oz.**	**398 mL**
Brown sugar, packed	**1 tbsp.**	**15 mL**
Fancy (mild) molasses	**1 tsp.**	**5 mL**
Ketchup	**¼ cup**	**60 mL**
Worcestershire sauce	**½ tsp.**	**2 mL**
Cocoa, sifted	**1 tbsp.**	**15 mL**

Fry onion in margarine in large saucepan until golden.

Add remaining 6 ingredients. Turn into ungreased 1 quart (1 L) casserole. Bake, uncovered, in 350°F (175°C) oven for about 35 minutes until hot and browning around outside edges. Makes 2 cups (500 mL).

1 serving: 151 Calories; 6 g Protein; 1.7 g Total Fat; 33 g Carbohydrate; 659 mg Sodium; 9 g Dietary Fiber

Pictured on page 117.

Ham Mole

Sauce also goes well with chicken.

Can of pitted cherries, with juice	**14 oz.**	**398 mL**
Apple cider vinegar	**2 tsp.**	**10 mL**
Ground cloves	**1/16 tsp.**	**0.5 mL**
Semisweet chocolate chips	**30**	**30**
Cornstarch	**1 tbsp.**	**15 mL**
Water	**2 tbsp.**	**30 mL**
Ham steak	**2¼ lbs.**	**1 kg**

Combine cherries with juice, vinegar, cloves and chocolate chips in medium saucepan. Heat, stirring occasionally, until boiling.

Mix cornstarch and water in small cup. Stir into cherry mixture until boiling and thickened.

Brown ham steak lightly on both sides. Serve with sauce over top or on side. Serves 6.

1 serving: 264 Calories; 33 g Protein; 7.7 g Total Fat; 14 g Carbohydrate; 2118 mg Sodium; 1 g Dietary Fiber

Pictured on page 117.

Meatloaf Mole

Looks great. Loaf holds together well. Cocoa enhances without flavoring.

Large eggs	**2**	**2**
Envelope of dry onion soup mix (1.4 oz., 38 g), stir before dividing	**½**	**½**
Water	**½ cup**	**125 mL**
Dry bread crumbs	**½ cup**	**125 mL**
Cocoa, sifted	**4 tsp.**	**20 mL**
Salt	**½ tsp.**	**2 mL**
Pepper	**¼ tsp.**	**1 mL**
Celery salt	**¼ tsp.**	**1 mL**
Lean ground beef	**2 lbs.**	**900 g**
Ketchup	**2 tbsp.**	**30 mL**

Beat eggs in large bowl. Add next 7 ingredients. Stir.

Mix in ground beef. Pack into ungreased 9 × 5 × 3 inch (22 × 12.5 × 7.5 cm) loaf pan.

Spread with ketchup. Bake in 350°F (175°C) oven for about 1¼ hours. Serves 8.

1 serving: 310 Calories; 24 g Protein; 18.9 g Total Fat; 10 g Carbohydrate; 833 mg Sodium; 1 g Dietary Fiber

Pictured on page 117.

Top Left: Meatloaf Mole, above
Top Right: Beans Mole, this page
Bottom: Ham Mole, this page

Chicken Mole

Serve this different dish to your next company. They'll never believe it contains chocolate.

Boneless, skinless chicken breast halves, pounded flat	6	6
Hard margarine	1 tbsp.	15 mL
Medium onion, chopped	1	1
Water	2 cups	500 mL
Can of diced green chilies, with liquid	4 oz.	114 mL
Toasted sliced almonds	1/3 cup	75 mL
Chicken bouillon powder	2 tsp.	10 mL
Chili powder	2 tsp.	10 mL
Granulated sugar	1 tsp.	5 mL
Salt	1 tsp.	5 mL
Pepper	1/4 tsp.	1 mL
Garlic powder (optional)	1/4 tsp.	1 mL
Ground cinnamon	1/8 tsp.	0.5 mL
Ground cloves, just a pinch		
Unsweetened chocolate baking square, cut up	1 oz.	28 g
Long grain white rice	1 1/3 cups	325 mL
Water	2 2/3 cups	650 mL
Salt	1/2 tsp.	2 mL
Medium tomatoes, seeded and diced	2	2

Brown chicken on both sides in margarine in frying pan. Remove to dish to keep warm.

Add onion to frying pan. Cook until golden.

Add next 12 ingredients. Stir. Add chicken. Cover. Simmer for 30 minutes until chicken is cooked. Remove chicken. Boil sauce, uncovered, for 10 minutes to thicken and reduce slightly. Slice chicken. Return to sauce.

Cook rice in second amounts of water and salt in covered medium saucepan for 15 to 20 minutes until tender and moisture is absorbed. Spread on platter. Spoon chicken mole over top.

Sprinkle with tomato. Serves 6.

1 serving: 390 Calories; 33 g Protein; 9.6 g Total Fat; 43 g Carbohydrate; 1140 mg Sodium; 3 g Dietary Fiber

Pictured on page 119.

Spareribs Mole

A dark sauce adds additional flavor to these tender ribs.

Pork spareribs, cut into 3 rib sections	3 lbs.	1.4 kg
Water, to cover		
Can of tomato sauce	7 1/2 oz.	213 mL
White vinegar	2 tsp.	10 mL
Brown sugar, packed	3 tbsp.	50 mL
Onion powder	1/2 tsp.	2 mL
Ground ginger	1/4 tsp.	1 mL
Garlic powder	1/4 tsp.	1 mL
Cocoa, sifted	1 tbsp.	15 mL
Liquid smoke	1/4 tsp.	1 mL

Cook spareribs in water for about 1 hour until tender. Drain. Spread on baking sheet with sides.

Combine remaining 8 ingredients in small saucepan. Boil, uncovered, until reduced and thickened. This will take about 10 minutes. Brush over ribs. Bake in 400°F (205°C) oven for 8 to 10 minutes. Turn ribs. Brush again with sauce. Bake for 8 to 10 minutes. Serves 6.

1 serving: 289 Calories; 21 g Protein; 20.3 g Total Fat; 5 g Carbohydrate; 297 mg Sodium; 1 g Dietary Fiber

Pictured on page 119.

Top: Spareribs Mole, above
Bottom: Chicken Mole, this page

Muffins & Breads

When the sweet aroma of melting chocolate mingles with the inviting warmth of freshly baked muffins or bread, you know that something special is happening in the kitchen. Even a simple bran muffin can be magically transformed with just a handful of chocolate chips. If you prefer sampling the flavor of chocolate in a more subtle presence, then you'll enjoy this collection of recipes.

Orange Chocolate Muffins are a welcome morning treat that you will want to turn into a habit. But don't stop there, because you just have to try Chocolate Mocha Loaf! If that isn't enough, then you'll be pleased to know that Chocolate Apple Fritters are only a few pages away, just waiting to be discovered.

As a convenience, all of these recipes can be frozen, except Choco Squigglies, *page 121.*

Choco Squigglies

These interesting-looking objects are best eaten fresh. Do not freeze.

Large egg	**1**	**1**
Milk	**7/8 cup**	**200 mL**
All-purpose flour	**1 cup**	**250 mL**
Cocoa, sifted	**1/4 cup**	**60 mL**
Granulated sugar	**2 tbsp.**	**30 mL**
Baking powder	**1 tsp.**	**5 mL**
Baking soda	**1/2 tsp.**	**2 mL**
Salt	**1/4 tsp.**	**1 mL**

Cooking oil, for deep-frying

Icing (confectioner's) sugar, for garnish

Beat egg in medium bowl. Add next 7 ingredients. Beat until smooth.

Pour batter into plastic squeeze bottle. Measure cooking oil into electric frying pan to depth of 1 inch (2.5 cm). Heat to 375°F (190°C). Squeeze batter into hot oil making spiral or zigzag pattern within about 3 inch (7 cm) diameter area. Cook for about 2 minutes, turning once, until puffed and browned. Remove with slotted spoon to paper towel.

Sprinkle with icing sugar. Serve warm. Makes about 12 squigglies.

1 squigglie: 80 Calories; 2 g Protein; 2.4 g Total Fat; 13 g Carbohydrate; 130 mg Sodium; 1 g Dietary Fiber

Pictured on this page.

Chocolate Scones

Served warm with butter, these make a good coffee treat.

All-purpose flour	1¾ cups	425 mL
Cocoa, sifted	⅓ cup	75 mL
Granulated sugar	¼ cup	60 mL
Baking powder	2 tsp.	10 mL
Baking soda	½ tsp.	2 mL
Salt	½ tsp.	2 mL
Hard margarine	¼ cup	60 mL
Semisweet chocolate chips	½ cup	125 mL
Large egg, fork-beaten	1	1
Milk	¾ cup	175 mL
Topping:		
Milk	1 tbsp.	15 mL
Granulated sugar, sprinkle, for garnish	1 tsp.	5 mL

Combine first 6 ingredients in large bowl. Add margarine. Cut in until crumbly.

Stir in chocolate chips, egg and milk to form soft ball. Knead on lightly floured surface 8 times. Divide into 2 equal portions. Pat each into 6 inch (15 cm) circle on greased baking sheet.

Topping: Brush tops with milk. Sprinkle with sugar. Score each top into 6 pie-shaped markings. Bake in 425°F (220°C) oven for about 15 minutes until risen and firm. Serve hot with butter. Makes 12 scones.

1 scone: 175 Calories; 4 g Protein; 7.3 g Total Fat; 25 g Carbohydrate; 237 mg Sodium; 2 g Dietary Fiber

Pictured on page 123.

Orange Chocolate Muffins

Light moist and delicate texture. Nicely shaped. Extra good.

All-purpose flour	2 cups	500 mL
Semisweet chocolate baking squares (1 oz., 28 g, each), grated	4	4
Baking powder	2 tsp.	10 mL
Baking soda	1 tsp.	5 mL
Salt	½ tsp.	2 mL
Hard margarine, softened	6 tbsp.	100 mL
Granulated sugar	¾ cup	175 mL
Large eggs	2	2
Grated peel of 1 medium orange		
Orange juice	¼ cup	60 mL
Buttermilk (or reconstituted from powder)	½ cup	125 mL

Measure first 5 ingredients into large bowl. Stir. Make a well.

Cream margarine and sugar in medium bowl. Beat in eggs, 1 at a time. Add orange peel, orange juice and buttermilk. Stir. Pour into well. Mix just to moisten. Fill greased muffin cups almost full. Bake in 400°F (205°C) oven for 15 to 20 minutes. A wooden pick inserted in center should come out clean. Let stand in pan for 5 minutes before removing to rack to cool. Makes 12 muffins.

1 muffin: 252 Calories; 4 g Protein; 10.4 g Total Fat; 37 g Carbohydrate; 323 mg Sodium; 2 g Dietary Fiber

Pictured on page 123.

Top Left: Orange Chocolate Muffins, above
Top Right: Chocolate Butter, page 110
Center Left: Chipper Muffins, page 124
Center Right: Banana Choco Muffins, page 124
Bottom Left: Chocolate Spread, page 113
Bottom Right: Chocolate Scones, this page

Chipper Muffins

Double the chocolate flavor with chocolate chips and cocoa. Great snacking!

All-purpose flour	**1¾ cups**	**425 mL**
Granulated sugar	**¾ cup**	**175 mL**
Cocoa, sifted	**⅓ cup**	**75 mL**
Baking powder	**1 tbsp.**	**15 mL**
Salt	**½ tsp.**	**2 mL**
Semisweet chocolate chips	**1 cup**	**250 mL**
Large egg	**1**	**1**
Cooking oil	**⅓ cup**	**75 mL**
Milk	**1 cup**	**250 mL**
Vanilla	**1 tsp.**	**5 mL**

Measure first 6 ingredients in medium bowl. Stir thoroughly. Make a well in center.

Beat egg in small bowl. Add cooking oil, milk and vanilla. Stir. Pour into well. Stir just to moisten. Fill greased muffin cups almost full. Bake in 400°F (205°C) oven for 15 to 20 minutes. A wooden pick inserted in center should come out clean. Let stand in pan for 5 minutes before removing to rack to cool completely. Makes 12 muffins.

1 muffin: 263 Calories; 4 g Protein; 11.8 g Total Fat; 38 g Carbohydrate; 136 mg Sodium; 3 g Dietary Fiber

Pictured on page 123.

Banana Choco Muffins

Using chunks of banana instead of mashed gives a burst of flavor in every good chocolate bite.

Hard margarine, softened	**6 tbsp.**	**100 mL**
Granulated sugar	**⅔ cup**	**150 mL**
Large eggs	**2**	**2**
Medium banana, diced	**1**	**1**
Milk	**⅔ cup**	**150 mL**
Vanilla	**½ tsp.**	**2 mL**
Chopped walnuts	**½ cup**	**125 mL**
All-purpose flour	**1¾ cups**	**425 mL**
Cocoa, sifted	**¼ cup**	**60 mL**
Baking powder	**2 tsp.**	**10 mL**
Baking soda	**½ tsp.**	**2 mL**
Mini semisweet chocolate chips	**½ cup**	**125 mL**

Cream margarine and sugar in large bowl. Beat in eggs, 1 at a time. Add banana, milk and vanilla. Stir to mix. Stir in walnuts.

Combine remaining 5 ingredients in medium bowl. Add to batter. Stir just to moisten. Fill greased muffin cups almost full. Bake in 400°F (205°C) oven for 15 to 20 minutes. A wooden pick inserted in center should come out clean. Let stand in pan for 5 minutes before removing to rack to cool completely. Makes 12 muffins.

1 muffin: 274 Calories; 5 g Protein; 13.1 g Total Fat; 36 g Carbohydrate; 154 mg Sodium; 2 g Dietary Fiber

Pictured on page 123.

Cranberry Chocolate Loaf

A rich chocolate contrast with tart red cranberries. A heavy, moist and delicious loaf.

Hard margarine, softened	1/2 cup	125 mL
Granulated sugar	1 cup	250 mL
Large eggs	2	2
Vanilla	1 tsp.	5 mL
Frozen cranberries, thawed and halved	1 1/4 cups	300 mL
Milk	3/4 cup	175 mL
All-purpose flour	2 cups	500 mL
Cocoa, sifted	1/3 cup	75 mL
Baking powder	1 tsp.	5 mL
Baking soda	1 tsp.	5 mL
Salt	1/4 tsp.	1 mL
Semisweet chocolate chips	1/2 cup	125 mL
Chopped walnuts	1/2 cup	125 mL

Cream margarine and sugar in large bowl. Beat in eggs, 1 at a time. Add vanilla, cranberries and milk. Stir.

Place remaining 7 ingredients in medium bowl. Stir. Add to batter. Mix just to moisten. Turn into greased 9 × 5 × 3 inch (22 × 12.5 × 7.5 cm) loaf pan. Bake in 350°F (175°C) oven for 65 to 70 minutes. A wooden pick inserted in center should come out clean. Let stand in pan for 10 minutes before turning out onto rack to cool completely. Cuts into 18 slices.

1 slice: 206 Calories; 4 g Protein; 10.1 g Total Fat; 27 g Carbohydrate; 192 mg Sodium; 2 g Dietary Fiber

Pictured on page 126/127.

Chocolate Mocha Loaf

This loaf has a rippled top like no other. A sprinkling of chocolate chips does the trick.

Hard margarine, softened	1/4 cup	60 mL
Granulated sugar	1 cup	250 mL
Large eggs	2	2
Vanilla	1 tsp.	5 mL
Milk	1 cup	250 mL
Instant coffee granules	1 tbsp.	15 mL
All-purpose flour	2 cups	500 mL
Cocoa, sifted	1/2 cup	125 mL
Baking powder	1 tbsp.	15 mL
Salt	3/4 tsp.	4 mL
Semisweet chocolate chips	1/4 cup	60 mL

Cream margarine and sugar in large bowl. Beat in eggs, 1 at a time. Stir in vanilla, milk and coffee granules.

Stir next 4 ingredients in medium bowl. Add to batter. Stir just to moisten. Turn into greased 9 × 5 × 3 inch (22 × 12.5 × 7.5 cm) loaf pan.

Sprinkle with chocolate chips. Bake in 350°F (175°C) oven for about 1 hour. A wooden pick inserted in center should come out clean. Let stand in pan for 10 minutes before turning out onto rack to cool completely. Cuts into 18 slices.

1 slice: 154 Calories; 3 g Protein; 4.5 g Total Fat; 27 g Carbohydrate; 163 mg Sodium; 2 g Dietary Fiber

Pictured on page 126/127.

Left: Chocolate Cherry Loaf, page 128
Center Left: Cranberry Chocolate Loaf, page 125
(baked in ribbed loaf pan)
Center Right: Chocolate Mocha Loaf, page 125
Right: Chocolate Zucchini Loaf, page 128

Chocolate Cherry Loaf

Both chocolate and cherry flavors come through well. A yummy, moist loaf.

Cream cheese, softened	4 oz.	125 g
Hard margarine, softened	½ cup	125 mL
Granulated sugar	1 cup	250 mL
Large eggs	3	3
Almond flavoring	½ tsp.	2 mL
All-purpose flour	1½ cups	375 mL
Cocoa, sifted	½ cup	125 mL
Baking powder	1½ tsp.	7 mL
Baking soda	½ tsp.	2 mL
Salt	¼ tsp.	1 mL
Sliced maraschino cherries	½ cup	125 mL

Beat cream cheese, margarine, sugar and 1 egg together in large bowl. Beat in remaining 2 eggs, 1 at a time. Stir in almond flavoring.

Add remaining 6 ingredients. Stir just to moisten. Turn into greased 9 × 5 × 3 inch (22 × 12.5 × 7.5 cm) loaf pan. Bake in 350°F (175°C) oven for about 1 hour. A wooden pick inserted in center should come out clean. Let stand in pan for 10 minutes before turning out onto rack to cool completely. Cuts into 18 slices.

1 slice: 181 Calories; 3 g Protein; 9 g Total Fat; 23 g Carbohydrate; 172 mg Sodium; 2 g Dietary Fiber

Pictured on page 126.

Chocolate Zucchini Loaf

Excellent flavor. Good choice.

Hard margarine, softened	½ cup	125 mL
Granulated sugar	1⅓ cups	325 mL
Large eggs	2	2
Vanilla	1 tsp.	5 mL
All-purpose flour	1¾ cups	425 mL
Cocoa, sifted	⅓ cup	75 mL
Baking soda	½ tsp.	2 mL
Baking powder	½ tsp.	2 mL
Salt	½ tsp.	2 mL
Grated zucchini, with peel, packed	1⅓ cups	325 mL
Sour milk (1 tsp., 5 mL, white vinegar plus milk)	⅓ cup	75 mL
Chopped walnuts (or pecans), optional	½ cup	125 mL

Cream margarine and sugar in medium bowl. Beat in eggs, 1 at a time. Stir in vanilla.

Stir flour, cocoa, baking soda, baking powder and salt in small bowl.

Stir zucchini and sour milk in separate small bowl. Add flour mixture to egg mixture in 3 parts, alternately with milk mixture in 2 parts, beginning and ending with flour mixture.

Stir in walnuts. Turn into greased 9 × 5 × 3 inch (22 × 12.5 × 7.5 cm) loaf pan. Bake in 350°F (175°C) oven for 70 to 80 minutes. A wooden pick inserted in center should come out clean. Let stand in pan for 10 minutes before turning out onto rack to cool completely. Cuts into 18 slices.

1 slice: 172 Calories; 3 g Protein; 6.3 g Total Fat; 27 g Carbohydrate; 188 mg Sodium; 2 g Dietary Fiber

Pictured on page 127.

Chocolate Doughnuts

Iced chocolate doughnuts are always a treat. Make extra special by adding sprinkles, tiny candies or toasted coconut.

Hard margarine, melted	2 tbsp.	30 mL
Granulated sugar	1 cup	250 mL
Large eggs	2	2
Milk	1 cup	250 mL
Vanilla	1 tsp.	5 mL
All-purpose flour	3½ cups	875 mL
Cocoa, sifted	½ cup	125 mL
Baking powder	4 tsp.	20 mL
Salt	½ tsp.	2 mL
Cooking oil, for deep-frying		
Chocolate Frosting:		
Hard margarine, softened	2 tbsp.	30 mL
Cocoa, sifted	⅓ cup	75 mL
Icing (confectioner's) sugar	1½ cups	375 mL
Water	3 tbsp.	50 mL
Vanilla	¾ tsp.	4 mL

Beat margarine, sugar and eggs together well in large bowl. Add milk and vanilla. Stir.

Add flour, cocoa, baking powder and salt. Mix well.

Roll out dough on lightly floured surface to ½ inch (12 mm) thick. Cut with 3 inch (7.5 cm) doughnut cutter. Drop carefully into hot 375°F (190°C) cooking oil, turning to cook both sides for 1½ minutes to 2 minutes per side. Cook center "holes" as well. Stand on edge on paper towel to drain.

Chocolate Frosting: Stir all 5 ingredients well in small bowl. Makes 1 cup (250 mL) frosting. Dip top side of doughnuts into frosting. Place on tray to set. Makes about 16 doughnuts.

1 frosted doughnut: 291 Calories; 5 g Protein; 8.5 g Total Fat; 51 g Carbohydrate; 137 mg Sodium; 3 g Dietary Fiber

Pictured on this page.

Chocolate Cinnamon Buns

Cocoa goes so well with cinnamon. The icing tops it off.

All-purpose flour	1 cup	250 mL
Cocoa, sifted	½ cup	125 mL
Instant yeast	1 tbsp.	15 mL
Granulated sugar	¼ cup	60 mL
Salt	1 tsp.	5 mL
Very warm water	1⅓ cups	325 mL
Cooking oil	¼ cup	60 mL
Large egg	1	1
All-purpose flour, approximately	2½ cups	625 mL
Filling:		
Hard margarine, softened	6 tbsp.	100 mL
Brown sugar, packed	1 cup	250 mL
Ground cinnamon	2 tbsp.	30 mL
Icing:		
Icing (confectioner's) sugar	1½ cups	375 mL
Hard margarine, softened	¼ cup	60 mL
Milk (or water)	3 tbsp.	50 mL
Vanilla	½ tsp.	2 mL

Measure first 5 ingredients into large bowl. Stir. Make a well.

Place water, cooking oil and egg into well. Beat on low to moisten. Beat on medium for about 2 minutes until smooth.

Work in enough remaining flour until dough leaves sides of bowl. Knead on lightly floured surface for 5 to 7 minutes until smooth and elastic. Divide dough into 4 equal portions. Roll 1 portion at a time ⅛ inch (3 mm) thick into 9 × 12 inch (22 × 30 cm) rectangle.

Filling: Spread each rectangle with 1½ tbsp. (25 mL) of margarine. Sprinkle with ¼ cup (60 mL) brown sugar and 1½ tsp. (7 mL) cinnamon. Roll up from long side like jelly roll. Cut into 1 inch (2.5 cm) slices. Place 24 slices, cut side down, in each of 2 greased 9 × 13 inch (22 × 33 cm) pans about ¼ to ½ inch (6 to 12 mm) apart. Cover with tea towel. Let stand in oven with light on and door closed for about 1 hour until doubled in size. Bake in 375°F (190°C) oven for 20 to 25 minutes. Turn out, bottom side up, onto rack to cool.

Icing: Beat all 4 ingredients together well in small bowl adding more icing sugar or milk to make a thin glaze. Invert buns. Drizzle with icing. Makes 48 buns.

1 bun: 110 Calories; 1 g Protein; 4 g Total Fat; 18 g Carbohydrate; 89 mg Sodium; 1 g Dietary Fiber

Pictured on page 131.

Chocolate Apple Fritters

Sprinkle these irregular shapes with icing sugar just before serving.

All-purpose flour	1⅔ cups	400 mL
Cocoa, sifted	⅓ cup	75 mL
Granulated sugar	3 tbsp.	50 mL
Baking powder	2 tsp.	10 mL
Ground cinnamon	½ tsp.	2 mL
Salt	¼ tsp.	1 mL
Large eggs	3	3
Hard margarine, melted	1 tbsp.	15 mL
Finely diced peeled cooking apples (such as McIntosh)	2 cups	500 mL
Semisweet chocolate chips	½ cup	125 mL
Cooking oil, for deep-frying		
Icing (confectioner's) sugar, for garnish		

Stir first 6 ingredients in large bowl. Make a well in center.

Beat eggs in small bowl until frothy and light in color. Pour into well. Add margarine, apple and chocolate chips. Stir just until moistened.

Drop, a few at a time, by rounded tablespoonfuls into hot 375°F (190°C) cooking oil. When starting to brown, use slotted spoon to turn. When both sides are browned, remove with slotted spoon to paper towel to drain. Cool completely.

Sprinkle with icing sugar. Makes 35 fritters.

1 fritter: 74 Calories; 1 g Protein; 4 g Total Fat; 9 g Carbohydrate; 30 mg Sodium; 1 g Dietary Fiber

Pictured on page 131.

Top: Chocolate Apple Fritters, above
Bottom: Chocolate Cinnamon Buns, this page
(with and without icing)

What cookbook would be complete without a classic selection of tried-and-true apple pie recipes? Well, maybe this one, because unless it has chocolate in it, it just isn't here! Take a distinguished dessert like pie, add a notable ingredient like chocolate, and there is no word to describe the absolutely wonderful result. Can you even begin to imagine what French Silk Pie will taste like? You'll just have to make it and find out for yourself.

Chocolate Quickie

A very last-minute dessert. Ready to serve in one hour. Whip this up just before meal preparation or just before coffee company comes.

Envelope of dessert topping (not prepared)	**1**	**1**
Milk	**½ cup**	**125 mL**
Vanilla	**½ tsp.**	**2 mL**
Instant chocolate pudding powder, 6 serving size	**1**	**1**
Milk	**1⅓ cups**	**325 mL**
Commercial 9 inch (22 cm) chocolate (or graham) crumb crust	**1**	**1**

Beat topping mix, first amount of milk and vanilla in small bowl until stiff.

Beat pudding powder and second amount of milk in medium bowl until smooth and thickened. Add topping. Fold in.

Turn into crumb crust. Chill for at least 1 hour. Cuts into 8 wedges.

1 wedge: 228 Calories; 4 g Protein; 7.2 g Total Fat; 38 g Carbohydrate; 483 mg Sodium; trace Dietary Fiber

Pictured on this page.

Double-Decker Pie

White layer is hidden underneath chocolate layer.

Crust:		
Hard margarine	1/3 cup	75 mL
Chocolate wafer crumbs	1 1/2 cups	375 mL
Filling:		
Light cream cheese, softened	8 oz.	250 g
Icing (confectioner's) sugar	3/4 cup	175 mL
Milk	1/4 cup	60 mL
Vanilla	1 tsp.	5 mL
Envelope of unflavored gelatin	1/4 oz.	7 g
Water	1/4 cup	60 mL
Semisweet chocolate baking squares (1 oz., 28 g, each), cut up	4	4
Envelope of dessert topping (not prepared)	1	1
Milk	1/2 cup	125 mL

Crust: Melt margarine in medium saucepan. Stir in wafer crumbs. Press in bottom and up sides of ungreased 9 inch (22 cm) pie plate. Bake in 350°F (175°C) oven for 10 minutes. Cool.

Filling: Beat first 4 ingredients in medium bowl until smooth.

Sprinkle gelatin over water in small saucepan. Let stand for 1 minute. Heat, stirring constantly, until dissolved. Whisk into batter. Measure 1/2 cup (125 mL) batter into small bowl.

Melt chocolate in medium saucepan over hot water, or on low, stirring constantly, until smooth. Do not overheat. Add to batter in small bowl. Stir well.

Beat topping mix and second amount of milk in separate small bowl until stiff. Fold 1/2 of dessert topping into chocolate batter. Fold second 1/2 of dessert topping into white batter. Turn white batter into prepared crust. Smooth chocolate mixture over top. Chill for several hours. Cuts into 8 wedges.

1 wedge: 397 Calories; 7 g Protein; 25.6 g Total Fat; 39 g Carbohydrate; 499 mg Sodium; 1 g Dietary Fiber

Pictured on page 134/135.

Double-Decker Pie, above (garnished with Chocolate Whipped Topping, page 109)

Chocolate Mousse Pie

Two-tone chocolate layers. Light texture.

Chocolate Pie Shell:		
Package pie crust mix (1/2 envelope)	**1 cup**	**250 mL**
Brown sugar, packed	**1/4 cup**	**60 mL**
Cocoa, sifted	**2 tbsp.**	**30 mL**
Water	**2 tbsp.**	**30 mL**
First Layer:		
Semisweet chocolate baking squares (1 oz., 28 g, each), cut up	**4**	**4**
Water	**2 tbsp.**	**30 mL**
Egg yolks (large)	**4**	**4**
Vanilla	**1 tsp.**	**5 mL**
Egg whites (large), room temperature	**4**	**4**
Granulated sugar	**1/3 cup**	**75 mL**
Second Layer:		
Hot water	**2 tbsp.**	**30 mL**
Cocoa, sifted	**2 tbsp.**	**30 mL**
Instant coffee granules	**2 tsp.**	**10 mL**
Vanilla	**1/2 tsp.**	**2 mL**
Milk, approximately	**1/2 cup**	**125 mL**
Envelope of dessert topping (not prepared)	**1**	**1**

Chocolate Pie Shell: Mix first 3 ingredients in medium bowl. Sprinkle with 1/2 of water. Toss with fork. Sprinkle with remaining water. Toss with fork. Form into flattened ball. Roll out on lightly floured surface. Line 9 inch (22 cm) pie plate with pastry, leaving 1/2 inch (12 mm) overhang. Poke holes with fork in bottom and sides of shell. Turn overhang under. Crimp edge. Bake in 425°F (220°C) oven for about 10 minutes. Cool.

First Layer: Heat chocolate and water in medium saucepan over hot water, or on low, stirring constantly, until smooth. Do not overheat. Remove from heat.

Add egg yolks and vanilla. Stir vigorously to blend. Cool.

Beat egg whites in large bowl until soft peaks form. Gradually add sugar, beating until stiff. Fold into cooled chocolate mixture. Turn into prepared pie shell. Bake on bottom rack in 350°F (175°C) oven for about 25 minutes until barely set. Let cool on rack for 1 hour. Chill well. Center will sink somewhat.

Second Layer: Stir hot water, cocoa and coffee granules in measuring cup until smooth. Set cup in 2 or 3 changes of ice water, stirring, until very cold.

Add vanilla and milk to make total of 1/2 cup (125 mL) liquid. Add topping mix. Beat until stiff. Spread over first layer. Chill. Cuts into 8 wedges.

1 wedge: 298 Calories; 6 g Protein; 15.2 g Total Fat; 38 g Carbohydrate; 160 mg Sodium; 2 g Dietary Fiber

Pictured on page 137.

Brownie Pie

Serve warm or cold with ice cream.

Hard margarine, softened	**1/2 cup**	**125 mL**
Brown sugar, packed	**1 cup**	**250 mL**
Large eggs	**2**	**2**
Vanilla	**1 tsp.**	**5 mL**
All-purpose flour	**2/3 cup**	**150 mL**
Cocoa, sifted	**1/2 cup**	**125 mL**
Salt	**1/4 tsp.**	**1 mL**
Chopped walnuts (optional)	**1/2 cup**	**125 mL**
Unbaked 9 inch (22 cm) pie shell	**1**	**1**

Cream margarine and brown sugar in large bowl. Mix in eggs, 1 at a time. Add vanilla. Stir.

Add flour, cocoa, salt and walnuts. Stir.

Turn into pie shell. Bake on bottom rack in 350°F (175°C) oven for 30 to 35 minutes. A wooden pick inserted in center should come out moist and a touch crumby. Serve warm or cooled. Cuts into 8 wedges.

1 wedge: 401 Calories; 5 g Protein; 21.5 g Total Fat; 50 g Carbohydrate; 391 mg Sodium; 3 g Dietary Fiber

Pictured on page 137.

Top Left: Brownie Pie, page 136
(garnished with Fudge Icing, page 110)
Bottom Right: Chocolate Mousse Pie, page 136

Mocha Crumb Pie

This pie has a chocolate crust on the bottom and in the middle. A delicious pie.

Mocha Crust:		
Hard margarine	**3/4 cup**	**175 mL**
Instant coffee granules	**3/4 tsp.**	**4 mL**
Chocolate wafer crumbs	**3 cups**	**750 mL**
Filling:		
Milk	**2 tbsp.**	**30 mL**
Instant coffee granules, crushed to a powder	**1 tsp.**	**5 mL**
Cream cheese, cut up	**4 oz.**	**125 g**
Semisweet chocolate chips	**2/3 cup**	**150 mL**
Envelope of dessert topping (not prepared)	**1**	**1**
Milk	**1/2 cup**	**125 mL**
Whipped topping, for garnish	**1 cup**	**250 mL**

Mocha Crust: Melt margarine and coffee granules in medium saucepan until coffee is dissolved.

Stir in wafer crumbs. Reserve 1 1/4 cups (300 mL) for middle and top. Press remaining mixture in bottom and up sides of ungreased 9 inch (22 cm) pie plate. Bake in 350°F (175°C) oven for 10 minutes. Cool.

Filling: Heat first amount of milk and coffee powder in medium saucepan, stirring often, until coffee is dissolved. Stir in cream cheese and chocolate chips until smooth and melted. Cool.

Beat topping mix and second amount of milk in small bowl until stiff. Fold about 1/4 into chocolate mixture. Fold remaining topping into chocolate mixture. Turn 1/2 of filling into prepared crust. Sprinkle with 3/4 cup (175 mL) reserved crumb mixture. Spoon remaining filling over top.

Garnish with whipped topping and remaining crumb mixture. Chill. Cuts into 8 wedges.

1 wedge: 478 Calories; 5 g Protein; 37.2 g Total Fat; 37 g Carbohydrate; 406 mg Sodium; 1 g Dietary Fiber

Pictured on page 139.

This recipe has stood the test of time.

Hard margarine, softened	**1/2 cup**	**125 mL**
Granulated sugar	**1 cup**	**250 mL**
Vanilla	**1 tsp.**	**5 mL**
Unsweetened chocolate baking squares (1 oz., 28 g, each), cut up	**3**	**3**
Large eggs	**3**	**3**
Baked 9 inch (22 cm) pie shell	**1**	**1**
Topping:		
Envelope of dessert topping (not prepared)	**1**	**1**
Milk	**1/2 cup**	**125 mL**
Vanilla	**1/2 tsp.**	**2 mL**

Cream margarine, sugar and vanilla in large bowl.

Melt chocolate in medium saucepan over hot water, or on low, stirring constantly, until smooth. Do not overheat. Beat into margarine mixture.

Add eggs, 1 at a time, beating on medium for 5 minutes after each addition, until thickened and smooth.

Turn into pie shell. Chill for 5 hours or more.

Topping: Beat topping mix, milk and vanilla in small bowl until stiff. Spoon over pie. Cuts into 8 wedges.

1 wedge: 445 Calories; 6 g Protein; 29.7 g Total Fat; 43 g Carbohydrate; 321 mg Sodium; 2 g Dietary Fiber

Pictured on page 139.

Top Left and Bottom: French Silk Pie, above (garnished with chocolate filigrees, page 24, and grated chocolate, page 19)
Center: Mocha Crumb Pie, this page (garnished with whipped topping)

Mud Pie

Incredibly good. A must-try. Dollops of whipped topping and chocolate-covered coffee beans make a great garnish.

Crust:		
Hard margarine	**1/3 cup**	**75 mL**
Chocolate wafer crumbs	**1 1/2 cups**	**375 mL**
Filling:		
Coffee ice cream, softened (see Note)	**1 1/2 qts.**	**1.5 L**
Fudge Sauce, page 153	**1/2 cup**	**125 mL**

Crust: Melt margarine in medium saucepan. Stir in wafer crumbs. Press in bottom and up sides of 9 inch (22 cm) pie plate. Bake in 350°F (175°C) oven for 10 minutes. Cool.

Filling: Pack ice cream evenly into crust. Freeze.

Spread fudge sauce evenly over ice cream. Freeze. Cuts into 8 wedges.

1 wedge: 444 Calories; 6 g Protein; 26.4 g Total Fat; 50 g Carbohydrate; 289 mg Sodium; 1 g Dietary Fiber

Pictured on page 141.

Note: If coffee ice cream isn't available, dissolve 1 tbsp. (15 mL) instant coffee granules in 2 tbsp. (30 mL) hot water. Mix into softened vanilla ice cream.

Mint Chiffon Pie

A light and airy pie. Pleasant flavor. A garnish of whipped topping tinted with green food coloring, gives a hint of the flavor to come.

Envelope of unflavored gelatin	**1/4 oz.**	**7 g**
Water	**1/4 cup**	**60 mL**
Water	**3/4 cup**	**175 mL**
Unsweetened chocolate baking squares (1 oz., 28 g, each), cut up	**2**	**2**
Egg yolks (large)	**3**	**3**
Granulated sugar	**1/2 cup**	**125 mL**
Peppermint flavoring	**1/2 tsp.**	**2 mL**
Salt	**1/4 tsp.**	**1 mL**
Egg whites (large), room temperature	**3**	**3**
Granulated sugar	**1/2 cup**	**125 mL**
Baked 9 inch (22 cm) pie shell	**1**	**1**

Sprinkle gelatin over first amount of water in small saucepan. Let stand for 1 minute. Heat, stirring constantly, until dissolved.

Combine second amount of water and chocolate in medium saucepan. Heat, stirring often, until chocolate is melted. Stir in gelatin.

Beat egg yolks in small bowl until light colored and increased in volume. Add first amount of sugar, peppermint flavoring and salt. Beat. Add to chocolate mixture. Heat and stir until just boiling. Remove from heat. Chill, stirring and scraping down sides occasionally, until thickened.

Beat egg whites in medium bowl until soft peaks form. Gradually beat in second amount of sugar until stiff. Fold into chocolate mixture.

Spoon into prepared pie shell. Chill for at least 2 hours. Cuts into 8 wedges.

1 wedge: 344 Calories; 5 g Protein; 18.3 g Total Fat; 43 g Carbohydrate; 253 mg Sodium; 1 g Dietary Fiber

Pictured on page 141.

Top Left: Mint Chiffon Pie, page 140
Bottom Right: Mud Pie, page 140

Meringue Chocolate Pie

A very tasty, showy pie with a very different crust.

Meringue Crust:		
Egg whites (large), room temperature	**3**	**3**
Cream of tartar	**1/4 tsp.**	**1 mL**
Salt	**1/16 tsp.**	**0.5 mL**
Granulated sugar	**3/4 cup**	**175 mL**
Butter cracker crumbs (such as Ritz)	**3/4 cup**	**175 mL**
Chopped pecans	**1/3 cup**	**75 mL**
Vanilla	**1/2 tsp.**	**2 mL**
Filling:		
Light cream cheese, softened	**4 oz.**	**125 g**
Granulated sugar	**1/3 cup**	**75 mL**
Milk	**2 tbsp.**	**30 mL**
Semisweet chocolate baking squares (1 oz., 28 g, each), cut up	**5**	**5**
Envelope of dessert topping (prepared according to package directions)	**1**	**1**

Meringue Crust: Beat first 3 ingredients in medium bowl until soft peaks form. Gradually beat in sugar, until stiff and sugar is dissolved.

Fold in next 3 ingredients. Spread in greased 9 inch (22 cm) pie plate pushing sides up higher than center. Bake in 325°F (160°C) oven for about 35 minutes until browned and dry. It may be slightly higher on the sides. Cool thoroughly.

Filling: Beat cream cheese, sugar and milk in medium bowl until smooth.

Melt chocolate in small saucepan over hot water, or on low, stirring constantly, until smooth. Do not overheat. Cool. Beat into cream cheese mixture.

Fold dessert topping into chocolate mixture. Spread over meringue shell. Chill for at least 3 hours. Cuts into 8 wedges.

1 wedge: 348 Calories; 6 g Protein; 19.1 g Total Fat; 49 g Carbohydrate; 308 mg Sodium; 2 g Dietary Fiber

Pictured on page 143.

Cherry White Chocolate Pie

This chilled dessert makes a very pretty ending to a dinner party.

Chocolate Graham Crust:		
Hard margarine	**1/3 cup**	**75 mL**
Graham cracker crumbs	**1 1/2 cups**	**375 mL**
Cocoa, sifted	**3 tbsp.**	**50 mL**
Filling:		
Spreadable non-fat cream cheese	**8 oz.**	**225 g**
Granulated sugar	**1/4 cup**	**60 mL**
Almond flavoring	**1/4 tsp.**	**1 mL**
White chocolate baking squares (1 oz., 28 g, each), cut up	**6**	**6**
Can of cherry pie filling, stir before dividing	**19 oz.**	**540 g**
Frozen light whipped topping, thawed	**1 cup**	**250 mL**

Chocolate Graham Crust: Melt margarine in medium saucepan. Stir in graham crumbs and cocoa. Press in bottom and up sides of ungreased 9 inch (22 cm) pie plate or heart-shaped pan. Bake in 350°F (175°C) oven for 10 minutes. Cool.

Filling: Beat cream cheese, sugar and flavoring in medium bowl until smooth and fluffy.

Heat chocolate in small saucepan over hot water, or on low, stirring constantly, until smooth. Do not overheat. Add to cream cheese mixture. Beat.

Fold in 2/3 of cherry pie filling. Fold in whipped topping. Spoon into prepared pie shell or heart-shaped pan. Spoon remaining pie filling around edge, keeping in from edge about 1 inch (2.5 cm). Serves 8.

1 wedge: 439 Calories; 6 g Protein; 18.6 g Total Fat; 65 g Carbohydrate; 261 mg Sodium; 2 g Dietary Fiber

Pictured on page 143.

Top: Cherry White Chocolate Pie, above
(in special heart-shaped pan)
Bottom: Meringue Chocolate Pie, this page

Creamy Chocolate Pie

A touch of cinnamon is in this winner.

Chocolate Pie Shell:		
All-purpose flour	1 cup	250 mL
Granulated sugar	$1\frac{1}{2}$ tbsp.	25 mL
Cocoa, sifted	$1\frac{1}{2}$ tbsp.	25 mL
Salt	$\frac{1}{4}$ tsp.	1 mL
Hard margarine	6 tbsp.	100 mL
Water	2 tbsp.	30 ml
Chocolate Filling:		
Granulated sugar	1 cup	250 mL
All-purpose flour	$\frac{1}{2}$ cup	125 mL
Cocoa, sifted	$\frac{1}{3}$ cup	75 mL
Egg yolks (large)	3	3
Milk	$2\frac{1}{2}$ cups	625 mL
Hard margarine	2 tbsp.	30 mL
Vanilla	1 tsp.	5 mL
Salt	$\frac{1}{8}$ tsp.	0.5 mL
Ground cinnamon	$\frac{1}{8}$ tsp.	0.5 mL
Meringue:		
Egg whites (large), room temperature	3	3
Cream of tartar	$\frac{1}{4}$ tsp.	1 mL
Granulated sugar	$\frac{1}{3}$ cup	75 mL

Chocolate Pie Shell: Combine first 4 ingredients in small bowl. Cut in margarine with pastry cutter until crumbly.

Sprinkle with water. Mix with fork to form a ball. Roll out on lightly floured surface. Fit into 9 inch (22 cm) pie plate, leaving $\frac{1}{2}$ inch (12 mm) overhang. Prick holes all over with fork. Turn overhang under. Crimp edge. Bake in 425°F (220°C) oven for about 10 minutes. Cool.

Chocolate Filling: Stir sugar, flour and cocoa well in medium saucepan.

Mix in egg yolks and a bit of milk. Add remaining milk. Heat, stirring often, until mixture boils and thickens. Remove from heat.

Add margarine, vanilla, salt and cinnamon. Stir. Pour into pie shell.

Meringue: Beat egg whites and cream of tartar in medium bowl until soft peaks form. Gradually beat in sugar, until mixture is stiff. Spread over filling being sure to touch edge of crust all around. Bake in 350°F (175°C) oven for about 10 minutes until browned. Cuts into 8 wedges.

1 wedge: 413 Calories; 9 g Protein; 15.1 g Total Fat; 64 g Carbohydrate; 343 mg Sodium; 3 g Dietary Fiber

Pictured on page 149.

Chocolate Pecan Pie

With a dark brown chocolaty and nutty filling. Add Chocolate Whipped Topping, page 109, for a finishing touch.

Large eggs	3	3
Brown sugar, packed	$\frac{3}{4}$ cup	175 mL
Dark corn syrup	$\frac{3}{4}$ cup	175 mL
Cocoa, sifted	3 tbsp.	50 mL
Vanilla	1 tsp.	5 mL
Pecans, halved or chopped	1 cup	250 mL
Unbaked 9 inch (22 cm) pie shell	1	1

Beat eggs in large bowl. Add brown sugar, corn syrup, cocoa and vanilla. Beat until smooth. Stir in pecans.

Turn into pie shell. Bake on bottom rack in 350°F (175°C) oven for 60 to 65 minutes. A knife inserted halfway between center and edge should come out clean. Cool. Cuts into 8 wedges.

1 wedge: 426 Calories; 5 g Protein; 20.1 g Total Fat; 60 g Carbohydrate; 190 mg Sodium; 2 g Dietary Fiber

Pictured on page 146.

Caramel Truffle Pie

Rich and sinful to be sure. Scrumptious.
Garnish topping with grated chocolate if desired.

Chocolate Crust:		
Hard margarine	**⅓ cup**	**75 mL**
Chocolate wafer crumbs	**1¼ cups**	**300 mL**
Finely chopped pecans	**½ cup**	**125 mL**
Icing (confectioner's) sugar	**1 tbsp.**	**15 mL**
Caramel Layer:		
Caramels	**20**	**20**
Hard margarine	**2 tbsp.**	**30 mL**
Milk	**2 tbsp.**	**30 mL**
Truffle Layer:		
Semisweet chocolate chips	**1½ cups**	**375 mL**
Envelope of dessert topping (prepared according to package directions)	**1**	**1**
Topping:		
Frozen light whipped topping, thawed	**2 cups**	**500 mL**

Chocolate Crust: Melt margarine in medium saucepan. Stir in wafer crumbs, pecans and icing sugar. Press in bottom and up sides of 9 inch (22 cm) pie plate. Bake in 350°F (175°C) oven for 10 minutes.

Caramel Layer: Heat caramels, margarine and milk in large saucepan, stirring often, until smooth. Pour into prepared crust. Cool completely.

Truffle Layer: Heat chocolate chips in medium saucepan over hot water, or on low, stirring constantly, until smooth. Do not overheat. Cool.

Fold dessert topping into chocolate. Spread over cooled caramel layer. Chill for 3 to 4 hours.

Topping: Spread whipped topping over pie. Cuts into 8 wedges.

1 wedge: 545 Calories; 5 g Protein; 37.3 g Total Fat; 55 g Carbohydrate; 278 mg Sodium; 3 g Dietary Fiber

Pictured on page 147.

Cheesy Chocolate Pie

Hard to tell which is better, the
crust or the filling. Tastes like a cheesecake.

Crust:		
All-purpose flour	**1½ cups**	**375 mL**
Finely chopped almonds	**¾ cup**	**175 mL**
Hard margarine	**¾ cup**	**175 mL**
Filling:		
Cream cheese, softened and cut up	**8 oz.**	**250 g**
Semisweet chocolate chips	**1 cup**	**250 mL**
Skim evaporated milk (or whipping cream)	**1 cup**	**250 mL**
Vanilla	**1 tsp.**	**5 mL**
Flake coconut	**½ cup**	**125 mL**

Crust: Process flour, almonds and margarine in food processor until mealy. Reserve ½ cup (125 mL). Press remaining flour mixture in bottom and up sides of 9 inch (22 cm) pie plate. Set aside.

Filling: Combine cream cheese, chocolate chips, evaporated milk and vanilla in medium saucepan. Heat on low, stirring often, until smooth. Remove from heat. Whisk or process in blender if necessary to smooth further.

Stir in coconut. Turn into prepared pie shell. Sprinkle reserved crumbs on top around edge. Bake in 350°F (175°C) oven for about 35 minutes. Cuts into 8 wedges.

1 wedge: 580 Calories; 11 g Protein; 44.9 g Total Fat; 38 g Carbohydrate; 353 mg Sodium; 3 g Dietary Fiber

Pictured on page 146 and 147.

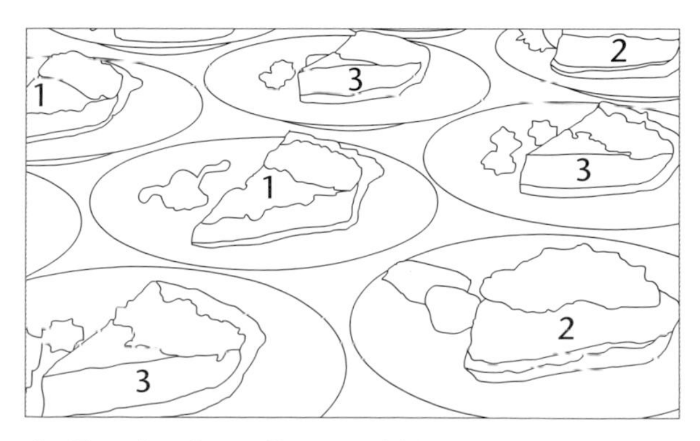

1. Chocolate Pecan Pie, page 144
2. Caramel Truffle Pie, this page
3. Cheesy Chocolate Pie, above

Turtle Pie

A decadent pie that's sure to please. Garnish with whipped topping and whole pecans. Or just serve with ice cream!

Semisweet chocolate chips	**1 cup**	**250 mL**
Skim evaporated milk	**3 tbsp.**	**50 mL**
Baked 9 inch (22 cm) pie shell	**1**	**1**
Caramels (about 32)	**9 oz.**	**252 g**
Skim evaporated milk	**1/3 cup**	**75 mL**
Chopped pecans, toasted	**1 cup**	**250 mL**
Skim evaporated milk	**1 tbsp.**	**15 mL**

Melt chocolate chips and first amount of evaporated milk in small saucepan over hot water, or on low, stirring constantly, until smooth. Do no overheat. Reserve 3 tbsp. (50 mL).

Spread remaining melted chocolate in bottom of pie shell. Chill well.

Melt caramels and second amount of evaporated milk in small saucepan, stirring constantly, until smooth. Pour over hardened chocolate layer.

Sprinkle with pecans. Pat down gently.

Stir reserved chocolate with third amount of evaporated milk. Drizzle in diamond pattern over all. Chill until caramel layer sets. Cuts into 8 wedges.

1 wedge: 450 Calories; 6 g Protein; 27.9 g Total Fat; 50 g Carbohydrate; 245 mg Sodium; 3 g Dietary Fiber

Pictured on page 149.

Nutty Chocolate Pie

Full of chewy things. Serve each wedge with a scoop of ice cream.

Large eggs	**3**	**3**
Hard margarine, melted	**1/2 cup**	**125 mL**
Granulated sugar	**1 1/4 cups**	**300 mL**
All-purpose flour	**1/2 cup**	**125 mL**
Vanilla	**1 tsp.**	**5 mL**
Semisweet chocolate chips	**1 cup**	**250 mL**
Chopped walnuts (or pecans)	**1 cup**	**250 mL**
Unbaked 9 inch (22 cm) pie shell	**1**	**1**

Beat eggs in medium bowl. Add margarine, sugar, flour and vanilla. Beat well.

Add chocolate chips and walnuts. Stir.

Turn into pie shell. Bake on bottom rack in 350°F (175°C) oven for about 45 minutes until set. Cuts into 8 wedges.

1 wedge: 598 Calories; 8 g Protein; 37.5 g Total Fat; 63 g Carbohydrate; 297 mg Sodium; 3 g Dietary Fiber

Pictured on page 149.

Top: Turtle Pie, this page
Center: Creamy Chocolate Pie, page 144
Bottom: Nutty Chocolate Pie, above

Chocolate Surprise Pie

The surprise is a hidden taste under the filling. Best eaten fresh.

Crust:		
Hard margarine	**⅓ cup**	**75 mL**
Graham cracker crumbs	**1¼ cups**	**300 mL**
Cocoa, sifted	**3 tbsp.**	**50 mL**
Raspberry or strawberry jam	**¾ cup**	**175 mL**
Cream cheese, softened	**4 oz.**	**125 g**
Granulated sugar	**½ cup**	**125 mL**
Milk	**1 cup**	**250 mL**
Instant chocolate pudding powder, 4 serving size	**1**	**1**
Envelope of dessert topping (not prepared)	**1**	**1**
Milk	**½ cup**	**125 mL**
Cocoa, sifted	**2 tbsp.**	**30 mL**
Vanilla	**½ tsp.**	**2 mL**

Crust: Melt margarine in medium saucepan. Add graham crumbs and cocoa. Stir well. Press in bottom and up sides of 9 inch (22 cm) pie plate. Bake in 350°F (175°C) oven for 10 minutes. Cool.

Spread raspberry jam in bottom of pie shell.

Beat cream cheese and sugar together well. Slowly beat in first amount of milk and pudding powder. Turn into cooled pie shell.

Beat topping mix and second amount of milk in small bowl until stiff. Beat in cocoa and vanilla. Pipe over top. Chill. Cuts into 8 wedges.

1 wedge: 439 Calories; 5 g Protein; 18.2 g Total Fat; 69 g Carbohydrate; 515 mg Sodium; 2 g Dietary Fiber

Pictured on page 151.

Chocolate Chess Pie

A soft chocolate and crunchy pecan filling. A Southern pie.

Large eggs	**2**	**2**
Granulated sugar	**1½ cups**	**375 mL**
Cocoa, sifted	**¼ cup**	**60 mL**
All-purpose flour	**1 tbsp.**	**15 mL**
Hard margarine, melted	**¼ cup**	**60 mL**
Milk	**½ cup**	**125 mL**
Vanilla	**1 tsp.**	**5 mL**
Salt	**⅛ tsp.**	**0.5 mL**
Chopped pecans (optional)	**½ cup**	**125 mL**
Unbaked 9 inch (22 cm) pie shell	**1**	**1**

Beat eggs in medium bowl until frothy. Beat in sugar, cocoa and flour. Add melted margarine, milk, vanilla and salt. Beat well.

Add pecans. Stir.

Turn into pie shell. Bake on bottom rack in 350°F (175°C) oven for 35 to 40 minutes until set. Cuts into 8 wedges.

1 wedge: 356 Calories; 4 g Protein; 15.4 g Total Fat; 53 g Carbohydrate; 278 mg Sodium; 2 g Dietary Fiber

Pictured on page 151.

Top: Chocolate Chess Pie, above (garnished with chocolate leaves, page 21, and orange slices)
Bottom: Chocolate Surprise Pie, this page (garnished with whipped topping and chocolate filigrees, page 24)

It's a magical elixir, that smooth, almost motionless chocolate sauce that creeps over ice cream or down the sides of a cheesecake. Not to be outdone by its cousin—icing, chocolate sauce offers a gentle touch of flavor on almost any kind of dessert, and also makes a wonderful dipping sauce. Chocolate sauce can even replace icing on a cake—a real feature for guests who would prefer to control how much chocolate goes on their dish. Simply offer it in a gravy boat or bowl, and let them indulge as they see fit.

Raspberry Coulis

Try koo-LEE for a picture-perfect dessert. A must with Chocolate Pâté, page 88.

Frozen raspberries in syrup, thawed	**15 oz.**	**425 g**
Granulated sugar	**2 tbsp.**	**30 mL**
Cornstarch	**4 tsp.**	**20 mL**

Strain raspberries through sieve. Reserve and measure syrup. Add water to make 1¼ cups (300 mL). Pour into saucepan.

Add sugar and cornstarch. Stir. Heat, stirring constantly, until mixture boils and thickens. Cool. Makes 1¼ cups (300 mL).

2 tbsp. (30 mL): 55 Calories; trace Protein; 0.1 g Total Fat; 14 g Carbohydrate; 1 mg Sodium; 2 g Dietary Fiber

Pictured on page 91 and page 98/99.

Strawberry Coulis

Use frozen sliced strawberries in syrup rather than raspberries.

Smooth Chocolate Sauce

Very easy-to-make sauce.

Cocoa, sifted	**1 cup**	**250 mL**
Granulated sugar	**½ cup**	**125 mL**
Corn syrup	**½ cup**	**125 mL**
Water	**1 cup**	**250 mL**
Vanilla	**1½ tsp.**	**7 mL**

Combine cocoa and sugar in medium saucepan. Stir in corn syrup and water. Heat, stirring constantly, until boiling. Simmer for 3½ minutes. Remove from heat.

Add vanilla. Stir. Makes 2 cups (500 mL).

2 tbsp. (30 mL): 67 Calories; 1 g Protein; 0.5 g Total Fat; 18 g Carbohydrate; 8 mg Sodium; 3 g Dietary Fiber

Pictured on page 43.

Hot Fudge Sauce

Very chocolaty, dark, thick and smooth. Excellent with Strawberry Sundae Cake, page 96.

Granulated sugar	**1 cup**	**250 mL**
Cocoa, sifted	**½ cup**	**125 mL**
Salt, pinch		
Evaporated milk	**⅔ cup**	**150 mL**
Butter (or hard margarine)	**¼ cup**	**60 mL**
Vanilla	**1 tsp.**	**5 mL**

Measure all 6 ingredients into heavy medium saucepan. Heat, stirring constantly, until mixture comes to a rolling boil that can't be stirred down. Start timing. Continue to stir for 1 minute. Remove from heat. Pour hot sauce over ice cream. Makes 1½ cups (375 mL).

2 tbsp. (30 mL): 351 Calories; 13 g Protein; 18.1 g Total Fat; 37 g Carbohydrate; 229 mg Sodium; 2 g Dietary Fiber

Pictured on page 97.

Fudge Sauce

Just meant for any ice cream dish. Use for Mud Pie, page 140.

Unsweetened chocolate baking squares (1 oz., 28 g, each), cut up	**4**	**4**
Evaporated milk	**¾ cup**	**175 mL**
Hard margarine	**2 tbsp.**	**30 mL**
Icing (confectioner's) sugar	**2 cups**	**500 mL**
Salt, just a pinch		
Vanilla	**½ tsp.**	**2 mL**

Combine first 5 ingredients in medium saucepan. Heat, stirring constantly, until boiling and chocolate is melted. Simmer on low for 5 minutes, stirring constantly.

Add vanilla. Stir. Makes 2 cups (500 mL).

2 tbsp. (30 mL): 376 Calories; 14 g Protein; 19.4 g Total Fat; 39 g Carbohydrate; 228 mg Sodium; trace Dietary Fiber

Pictured on page 141.

Amaretto Choco Sauce

Good chocolate sauce without being too sweet.

Unsweetened chocolate baking squares (1 oz., 28 g, each), cut up	**6**	**6**
Evaporated milk	**¾ cup**	**175 mL**
Granulated sugar	**⅔ cup**	**150 mL**
Amaretto liqueur	**3 tbsp.**	**50 mL**

Heat chocolate, evaporated milk and sugar in medium saucepan on low, stirring often, until smooth and sugar is dissolved. Remove from heat.

Add Amaretto. Stir. Makes 2 cups (500 mL).

2 tbsp. (30 mL): 369 Calories; 15 g Protein; 21.2 g Total Fat; 33 g Carbohydrate; 213 mg Sodium; 2 g Dietary Fiber

Pictured on page 155.

White Chocolate Sauce

This is good with or without the chocolate flavoring which does add a caramel color. Wonderful served over fresh berries.

White chocolate baking squares (1 oz., 28 g, each), cut up	**6**	**6**
Skim evaporated milk	**½ cup**	**125 mL**
White corn syrup	**1 tbsp.**	**15 mL**
Vanilla (white is best)	**½ tsp.**	**2 mL**
Chocolate flavoring (optional)	**½ tsp.**	**2 mL**

Combine all 5 ingredients in medium saucepan. Heat on low, stirring often, until melted and smooth. Makes 1¼ cups (300 mL).

2 tbsp. (30 mL): 109 Calories; 2 g Protein; 5.2 g Total Fat; 13 g Carbohydrate; 31 mg Sodium; 0 g Dietary Fiber

Pictured on page 155.

Kids' Cola Sauce

A novel sauce kids will like. Serve over biscuits, pancakes or ice cream.

Granulated sugar	**⅓ cup**	**75 mL**
Cocoa, sifted	**3 tbsp.**	**50 mL**
Cornstarch	**1 tbsp.**	**15 mL**
Salt, just a pinch		
Cola soft drink	**¾ cup**	**175 mL**
Milk	**½ cup**	**125 mL**

Combine sugar, cocoa, cornstarch and salt in medium saucepan.

Stir in soft drink until moistened. Add milk. Heat, stirring constantly, until boiling and thickened. Makes 1⅓ cups (325 mL).

2 tbsp. (30 mL): 42 Calories; 1 g Protein; 0.2 g Total Fat; 10 g Carbohydrate; 7 mg Sodium; 1 g Dietary Fiber

Pictured on page 155.

Variation: For a less cola flavor add ½ cup (125 mL) water and only ¼ cup (60 mL) cola.

Peanut Fudge Sauce

Delicious over ice cream. A favorite. For a thinner sauce, stir in a bit more milk.

Sweetened chocolate drink powder	**1 cup**	**250 mL**
Milk	**2 tbsp.**	**30 mL**
Smooth peanut butter	**1 tbsp.**	**15 mL**

Combine all 3 ingredients in small saucepan. Heat, stirring constantly, until blended smooth. Cool. Pour into jar. Sauce thickens as it stands. Makes ¾ cup (175 mL).

2 tbsp. (30 mL): 118 Calories; 2 g Protein; 2.2 g Total Fat; 27 g Carbohydrate; 75 mg Sodium; trace Dietary Fiber

Pictured on page 155.

Top Left: Kids' Cola Sauce, this page
Center Left: White Chocolate Sauce, this page
Center Right: Peanut Fudge Sauce, this page
Bottom: Amaretto Choco Sauce, this page

Squares

It begins with the classic, much-loved Brownie.
No square is more recognized or revered by chocolate lovers.
A chocolate Brownie and a glass of milk can comfort the
soul like a bowl of chicken soup never could.
Of course, you will find the perfect recipe
for Brownies in this section. But don't forget to also
consider some other great chocolate-filled recipes, like
Fudge Crispies or Chocolate Magic Squares. Make up a selection
and pop them in the freezer. When someone needs a little comforting
you'll be ready. It's always a treat to bring some cheer
into your life, one square at a time!

Candy Bar Squares

This can also be served as candy. Either way, it is really good. Tastes like a famous chocolate bar.

Semisweet chocolate chips	2 cups	500 mL
Peanut butter chips	1 cup	250 mL
Hard margarine	1/3 cup	75 mL
Milk	1/3 cup	75 mL
Granulated sugar	1 1/4 cups	300 mL
Coarsely chopped salted peanuts	3/4 cup	175 mL
Smooth peanut butter	1/4 cup	60 mL
Marshmallow crème	1 cup	250 mL
Vanilla	1 tsp.	5 mL
Coarsely chopped salted peanuts	3/4 cup	175 mL
Caramels	40	40
Water	2 1/2 tbsp.	37 mL

Heat both chips in large saucepan over hot water, or on low, stirring constantly, until smooth. Do not overheat. Spread half of mixture in greased or foil-lined 9 × 13 inch (22 × 33 cm) pan. Cool thoroughly.

Heat margarine, milk and sugar in medium saucepan, stirring often, until boiling. Boil for 5 minutes, stirring often. Pour over cooled layer in pan.

Sprinkle with first amount of peanuts.

Heat and stir peanut butter in small saucepan until melted. Remove from heat. Stir in marshmallow crème and vanilla until smooth. Spoon in dabs over peanuts.

Sprinkle with second amount of peanuts.

Heat caramels and water in medium saucepan, stirring often, until smooth. Drizzle and spread over peanuts. Reheat remaining half of chocolate mixture if necessary. Spoon and spread over caramel. Chill thoroughly. Cuts into 54 squares.

2 squares: 135 Calories; 2 g Protein; 6.4 g Total Fat; 20 g Carbohydrate; 70 mg Sodium; 1 g Dietary Fiber

Pictured on this page.

Oven S'Mores

S'more, please!

Hard margarine, softened	**½ cup**	**125 mL**
Brown sugar, packed	**½ cup**	**125 mL**
Graham cracker crumbs	**¾ cup**	**175 mL**
All-purpose flour	**¾ cup**	**175 mL**
Semisweet chocolate chips	**1 cup**	**250 mL**
Miniature marshmallows	**2 cups**	**500 mL**

Cream margarine and brown sugar in medium bowl until fluffy.

Stir in graham crumbs and flour. Press in greased or foil-lined 9 x 9 inch (22 x 22 cm) pan. Bake in 350°F (175°C) oven for 10 minutes. Reduce oven heat to 250°F (120°C).

Sprinkle with ½ of chocolate chips and all marshmallows. Sprinkle with second ½ of chocolate chips. Bake in 250°F (120°C) oven for 10 to 12 minutes until marshmallows are puffed and melted. Broil for about 1 minute to brown lightly, watching carefully. Cuts into 36 squares.

1 square: 85 Calories; 1 g Protein; 4.4 g Total Fat; 12 g Carbohydrate; 52 mg Sodium; trace Dietary Fiber

Pictured on page 159.

Crisp Candy Squares

A sweet and crunchy goody.

Semisweet chocolate chips	**1 cup**	**250 mL**
Smooth peanut butter	**½ cup**	**125 mL**
Crisp rice cereal	**1½ cups**	**375 mL**
Peanuts, chopped (optional)	**½ cup**	**125 mL**

Melt chocolate chips and peanut butter in medium saucepan over hot water, or on low, stirring constantly, until melted and smooth.

Stir in rice cereal and peanuts. Pack into greased or foil-lined 8 x 8 inch (20 x 20 cm) pan. Chill. Cuts into 25 squares.

1 square: 68 Calories; 2 g Protein; 4.8 g Total Fat; 6 g Carbohydrate; 45 mg Sodium; 1 g Dietary Fiber

Pictured on page 163.

Fudge Crispies

Crunchy and good dark chocolate flavor.

Semisweet chocolate chips	**2 cups**	**500 mL**
Hard margarine	**½ cup**	**125 mL**
Corn syrup	**½ cup**	**125 mL**
Vanilla	**2 tsp.**	**10 mL**
Icing (confectioner's) sugar	**1 cup**	**250 mL**
Crisp rice cereal	**4 cups**	**1 L**

Put first 4 ingredients into large saucepan. Heat on low, stirring often, until chips are melted.

Stir in icing sugar.

Measure cereal into large bowl. Add chocolate mixture. Stir well to coat. Pack into greased or foil-lined 9 x 9 inch (22 x 22 cm) pan. Let stand until firm. Cuts into 36 squares.

1 square: 106 Calories; 1 g Protein; 5.7 g Total Fat; 15 g Carbohydrate; 71 mg Sodium; 1 g Dietary Fiber

Pictured on page 159.

Mars Bars Squares

Crisp and chocolaty. For a pretty contrast, drizzle melted white chocolate over top before cutting.

Mars candy bars (2 oz., 58 g, each, black and red label), cut up	**4**	**4**
Hard margarine	**½ cup**	**125 mL**
Crisp rice cereal	**3 cups**	**750 mL**
Topping:		
Semisweet chocolate chips	**1 cup**	**250 mL**
Hard margarine	**¼ cup**	**60 mL**

Heat candy bars and margarine in large saucepan on low, stirring constantly, until melted and well combined. Remove from heat.

Add rice cereal. Stir to coat. Pack into greased or foil-lined 9 x 9 inch (22 x 22 cm) pan.

Topping: Heat both ingredients in small saucepan, stirring often, until smooth. Spread over top. Cool. Cuts into 36 squares.

1 square: 90 Calories; 1 g Protein; 6.3 g Total Fat; 9 g Carbohydrate; 86 mg Sodium; trace Dietary Fiber

Pictured on page 159.

Top: Fudge Crispies, this page
Center: Oven S'Mores, this page
Bottom: Mars Bars Squares, this page

Crusty Brownies

Brownies rest on a rolled oat base.

First Layer:		
Hard margarine	**3/4 cup**	**175 mL**
Quick-cooking rolled oats (not instant)	**1 1/2 cups**	**375 mL**
All-purpose flour	**1 cup**	**250 mL**
Brown sugar, packed	**1 cup**	**250 mL**
Baking soda	**3/4 tsp.**	**4 mL**
Salt	**1/4 tsp.**	**1 mL**
Second Layer:		
Hard margarine	**1/2 cup**	**125 mL**
Unsweetened chocolate baking squares (1 oz., 28 g, each), cut up	**2**	**2**
Granulated sugar	**1 1/2 cups**	**375 mL**
Large eggs	**2**	**2**
Milk	**1/2 cup**	**125 mL**
Vanilla	**1 1/2 tsp.**	**7 mL**
All-purpose flour	**1 1/3 cups**	**325 mL**
Chopped walnuts (or pecans)	**3/4 cup**	**175 mL**
Creamy Chocolate Frosting, page 111		

First Layer: Melt margarine in medium saucepan.

Combine next 5 ingredients in medium bowl. Add margarine. Stir. Press in greased or foil-lined 9 × 13 inch (22 × 33 cm) pan. Bake in 350°F (175°C) oven for 10 to 12 minutes.

Second Layer: Melt margarine and chocolate in large saucepan on low, stirring often, until smooth.

Add sugar and eggs. Beat until blended. Stir in milk and vanilla.

Add flour and walnuts. Stir. Spread over first layer. Bake in 350°F (175°C) oven for 30 to 35 minutes. A wooden pick inserted in center should come out moist but clean. Cool.

Spread with frosting. Cuts into 54 squares.

1 square: 162 Calories; 2 g Protein; 9.1 g Total Fat; 20 g Carbohydrate; 105 mg Sodium; 1 g Dietary Fiber

Pictured on page 162/163.

Butterscotch Chip Squares

A brownie-like base with two kinds of chips.

Butterscotch chips	**1/2 cup**	**125 mL**
Cooking oil	**1/4 cup**	**60 mL**
All-purpose flour	**3/4 cup**	**175 mL**
Brown sugar, packed	**1/2 cup**	**125 mL**
Vanilla	**1/2 tsp.**	**2 mL**
Salt	**1/16 tsp.**	**0.5 mL**
Large egg	**1**	**1**
Miniature marshmallows	**1 cup**	**250 mL**
Semisweet chocolate chips	**1/2 cup**	**125 mL**

Heat butterscotch chips and cooking oil in large saucepan on low, stirring constantly, until chips are melted.

Mix in flour, brown sugar, vanilla and salt. Add egg. Stir vigorously.

Stir in remaining 2 ingredients. Press in greased or foil-lined 9 × 9 inch (22 × 22 cm) pan. Bake in 350°F (175°C) oven for 20 to 25 minutes. Wooden pick inserted near center should come out moist but clean. Cuts into 36 squares.

1 square: 61 Calories; 1 g Protein; 2.6 g Total Fat; 9 g Carbohydrate; 10 mg Sodium; trace Dietary Fiber

Pictured on page 162.

Hint O' Mint Squares

The final result is a ribbon of green through the square.

Hard margarine, softened	1/4 cup	60 mL
Peppermint flavoring	1/2 tsp.	2 mL
Icing (confectioner's) sugar	1 cup	250 mL
Drops of green food coloring	2	2
Hard margarine	1/2 cup	125 mL
Granulated sugar	1/4 cup	60 mL
Cocoa, sifted	1/4 cup	60 mL
Large egg, fork-beaten	1	1
Chocolate wafer crumbs	3/4 cup	175 mL
Graham cracker crumbs	3/4 cup	175 mL
Flake coconut	3/4 cup	175 mL
Semisweet chocolate chips	3/4 cup	175 mL
Hard margarine, melted	2 1/2 tbsp.	37 mL

Beat first amount of margarine, flavoring, icing sugar and food coloring in small bowl until smooth. Pack mixture in waxed paper-lined 9 × 9 inch (22 × 22 cm) pan. Freeze.

Heat and stir second amount of margarine, sugar and cocoa in large saucepan until simmering and sugar is dissolved. Remove from heat. Quickly whisk in egg to thicken slightly.

Stir in both crumbs and coconut until moistened. Crumble half of mixture into ungreased or foil-lined 9 × 9 inch (22 × 22 cm) pan, but don't pack. Remove peppermint layer from freezer. Remove from pan. Turn upside down on top of chocolate. Peel off waxed paper. No problem if crust breaks or is uneven. Crumble remaining half of chocolate mixture over top. Pack firmly into pan.

Melt chocolate chips and third amount of margarine in small saucepan over hot water, or on low, stirring constantly, until smooth. Pour over squares. Spread evenly. Let stand until chocolate is firm. Cuts into 36 squares.

1 square: 114 Calories; 1 g Protein; 8.2 g Total Fat; 11 g Carbohydrate; 85 mg Sodium; 1 g Dietary Fiber

Pictured on this page.

Left: Butterscotch Chip Squares, page 160
Top Center: Crusty Brownies, page 160
Right: Crisp Candy Squares, page 158

Marbled Brownies

A soft and thick square. Self-iced.

Hard margarine	**½ cup**	**125 mL**
Unsweetened chocolate baking squares (1 oz., 28 g, each), cut up	**2**	**2**
Large eggs	**2**	**2**
Granulated sugar	**1 cup**	**250 mL**
Vanilla	**½ tsp.**	**2 mL**
All-purpose flour	**¾ cup**	**175 mL**
Salt	**¼ tsp.**	**1 mL**
Chopped walnuts (optional)	**½ cup**	**125 mL**
Marble Filling:		
Cream cheese, softened	**4 oz.**	**125 g**
Granulated sugar	**½ cup**	**125 mL**
Large egg	**1**	**1**
Vanilla	**½ tsp.**	**2 mL**

Melt margarine and chocolate in small saucepan over hot water, or on low, stirring constantly, until smooth. Do not overheat.

Beat eggs in large bowl until frothy. Add sugar and vanilla. Mix. Add chocolate mixture. Stir.

Add flour, salt and walnuts. Stir to moisten. Spread in greased or foil-lined 9 × 9 inch (22 × 22 cm) pan.

Marble Filling: Beat all 4 ingredients in small bowl until smooth. Drop dabs here and there over chocolate mixture. Use knife to make zigzag pattern. Do not overmix. (See Marbling, page 23). Bake in 350°F (175°C) oven for about 45 minutes. Wooden pick inserted in center should come out moist but clean. Cuts into 25 squares.

1 square: 136 Calories; 2 g Protein; 7.5 g Total Fat; 16 g Carbohydrate; 90 mg Sodium; trace Dietary Fiber

Pictured on page 165.

Cracker Candy Squares

Soft and chewy. Dust with icing sugar, if desired.

Graham cracker crumbs (see Note)	**2½ cups**	**625 mL**
Sweetened condensed milk	**11 oz.**	**312 mL**
Semisweet chocolate chips	**2 cups**	**500 mL**

Mix all 3 ingredients in medium bowl. Press in greased or foil-lined 9 × 13 inch (22 × 33 cm) pan. Bake in 350°F (175°C) oven for 25 to 30 minutes. Cuts into 54 squares.

1 serving: 72 Calories; 1 g Protein; 3.1 g Total Fat; 11 g Carbohydrate; 46 mg Sodium; trace Dietary Fiber

Pictured on page 165.

Note: Use 3 cups (750 mL) crumbs if using a 14 oz. (398 mL) can of condensed milk.

Cookie Brownies

A shortbread crust with a brownie top. Sweetened condensed milk adds its flavor.

Crust:		
All-purpose flour	**1½ cups**	**375 mL**
Granulated sugar	**¼ cup**	**60 mL**
Hard margarine, softened	**¾ cup**	**175 mL**
Topping:		
Can of sweetened condensed milk (or 14 oz., 398 mL)	**11 oz.**	**300 mL**
Large egg	**1**	**1**
Cocoa, sifted	**½ cup**	**125 mL**
All-purpose flour	**¼ cup**	**60 mL**
Vanilla	**1 tsp.**	**5 mL**
Chopped walnuts	**¾ cup**	**175 mL**
Hot water	**2 tbsp.**	**30 mL**
Instant coffee granules	**1 tsp.**	**5 mL**

Crust: Mix flour, sugar and margarine in medium bowl until crumbly. Press in ungreased or foil-lined 9 × 13 inch (22 × 33 cm) pan. Bake in 350°F (175°C) oven for about 15 minutes.

Topping: Stir first 6 ingredients together in medium bowl.

Stir hot water into coffee granules in cup. Add to milk mixture. Stir. Spread over crust. Bake for 20 to 25 minutes until set. Cool thoroughly. Cuts into 54 squares.

1 square: 83 Calories; 2 g Protein; 4.7 g Total Fat; 9 g Carbohydrate; 43 mg Sodium; 1 g Dietary Fiber

Pictured on page 165.

Top: Cracker Candy Squares, this page
Center: Marbled Brownies, this page
Bottom: Cookie Brownies, this page

Chocolate Magic Squares

This will please every sweet tooth out there.

Hard margarine	1/4 cup	60 mL
Crushed chocolate cream-filled cookies (about 24)	2 cups	500 mL
Sweetened condensed milk (or 14 oz., 398 mL)	11 oz.	300 mL
Semisweet chocolate chips	1 cup	250 mL
Vanilla	1 tsp.	5 mL
Chopped walnuts	3/4 cup	175 mL
Semisweet chocolate chips	1 cup	250 mL

Melt margarine in small saucepan. Stir in crushed cookies. Press in ungreased or foil-lined 9 x 13 inch (22 x 33 cm) pan. Set aside.

Combine condensed milk, first amount of chocolate chips and vanilla in medium saucepan. Heat on low, stirring often, until chips are melted. Pour into prepared crust.

Sprinkle with walnuts and second amount of chocolate chips. Bake in 350°F (175°C) oven for 25 minutes until set. Cool. Cuts into 54 squares.

1 square: 94 Calories; 1 g Protein; 5.7 g Total Fat; 11 g Carbohydrate; 43 mg Sodium; trace Dietary Fiber

Pictured on page 167.

Colored Mallow Squares

Always freezer-ready and so good.

Hard margarine	6 tbsp.	100 mL
Semisweet chocolate chips	3/4 cup	175 mL
Peanut butter chips	3/4 cup	175 mL
Smooth peanut butter	1/4 cup	60 mL
Miniature colored marshmallows, lightly packed	5 cups	1.25 L

Melt margarine in large saucepan. Add both chips and peanut butter. Heat on low, stirring often, until smooth. Remove from heat.

Add marshmallows. Stir well to coat. Press in ungreased or foil-lined 9 x 9 inch (22 x 22 cm) pan. Chill. Cuts into 36 squares.

1 square: 79 Calories; 1 g Protein; 4.3 g Total Fat; 10 g Carbohydrate; 42 mg Sodium; trace Dietary Fiber

Pictured on page 167.

Peanut Butter Squares

A melt-in-your-mouth square!

First Layer:		
Hard margarine	1/2 cup	125 mL
Smooth peanut butter	1/2 cup	125 mL
Icing (confectioner's) sugar	2 cups	500 mL
Graham cracker crumbs	1/3 cup	75 mL
Top Layer:		
Granulated sugar	1/2 cup	125 mL
Water	3 tbsp.	50 mL
Hard margarine	2 tbsp.	30 mL
Semisweet chocolate chips	1/2 cup	125 mL

First Layer: Melt margarine and peanut butter in medium saucepan. Mix in icing sugar and graham crumbs. Pack in ungreased or foil-lined 8 x 8 inch (20 x 20 cm) pan.

Top Layer: Combine sugar, water and margarine in medium saucepan. Heat, stirring often, until boiling. Boil for 1 minute.

Add chocolate chips. Stir to melt. Pour over first layer. Chill well. Cuts into 25 squares.

1 square: 150 Calories; 2 g Protein; 8.8 g Total Fat; 17 g Carbohydrate; 93 mg Sodium; 1 g Dietary Fiber

Pictured on page 167.

Top: Colored Mallow Squares, page 166
Center Right: Peanut Butter Squares, page 166
Bottom Left: Chocolate Magic Squares, page 166

The ultimate chocolate fantasy is right here at your fingertips,
a classic selection of some of the most well-known recipes made easy-to-follow.
From Chocolate Crêpes to Black And White Eclairs and Chocolate Cream Puffs—it's all here
in these pages, just waiting for your attention. Have some creative fun making delicate
Chocolate Cups, and fill them with delicious Chocolate Mocha Mousse or Chantilly Butter Crunch.
Were you looking for the perfect candlelight dessert or perhaps an impressive ending
to a dinner with your in-laws? Well, don't just impress—dazzle!

Special Touches

Chocolate Crêpes

Stack crêpes in desired numbers and wrap well. Freeze for up to 3 months. Recipe doubles easily.

Large eggs	**2**	**2**
Milk	**3/4 cup**	**175 mL**
Water	**2/3 cup**	**150 mL**
All-purpose flour	**1 cup**	**250 mL**
Cocoa, sifted	**2 tbsp.**	**30 mL**
Cooking oil	**2 tbsp.**	**30 mL**
Granulated sugar	**3 tbsp.**	**50 mL**
Vanilla	**1/2 tsp.**	**2 mL**
Salt	**1/16 tsp.**	**0.5 mL**

Beat eggs in medium bowl. Add remaining 8 ingredients. Beat until smooth. Let stand for 1 hour to let air bubbles rise and settle.

1. Heat lightly sprayed 8 inch (20 cm) non-stick frying pan on medium. Quickly pour 1½ tbsp. (25 mL) batter into hot pan. Swirl immediately so batter covers bottom of pan. Heat for about 1 minute until underside is lightly browned.

2. Using rubber spatula to loosen edges, turn out of pan onto waxed paper. Makes 24 crêpes.

1 unfilled crêpe: 47 Calories; 1 g Protein; 1.8 g Total Fat; 7 g Carbohydrate; 16 mg Sodium; trace Dietary Fiber

Pictured on page 170/171.

Chocolate Cream Crêpes

The two-layered filling makes a pretty presentation.

Envelope dessert topping (not prepared)	**1**	**1**
Milk	**1/2 cup**	**125 mL**
Vanilla	**1/2 tsp.**	**2 mL**
Semisweet chocolate chips	**1/3 cup**	**75 mL**
Granulated sugar	**2 tbsp.**	**30 mL**
Milk	**1 cup**	**250 mL**
Salt, just a pinch		
Cornstarch	**1 tbsp.**	**15 mL**
Water	**1 tbsp.**	**15 mL**
Vanilla	**1 tsp.**	**5 mL**
Rum flavoring	**1 tsp.**	**5 mL**
Chocolate Crêpes, this page	**8**	**8**

Beat dessert topping and first amounts of milk and vanilla in small bowl until stiff. Chill.

Combine chocolate chips, sugar, second amount of milk and salt in medium saucepan. Heat on medium-low, stirring often, until smooth and simmering.

Mix cornstarch and water in small cup. Add to chocolate mixture, stirring constantly, until thickened.

Stir in second amount of vanilla and rum flavoring. Cool.

Spread about 2 tbsp. (30 mL) chocolate mixture on each crêpe. Spoon or pipe about 3 to 4 tbsp. (50 to 60 mL) topping down center over chocolate. Fold both sides of crêpe over topping. Spoon remaining chocolate mixture over crêpes.

2 filled crêpes: 295 Calories; 7 g Protein; 13.1 g Total Fat; 39 g Carbohydrate; 95 mg Sodium; 2 g Dietary Fiber

Pictured on page 170/171.

Ice-Cream Crêpes

A great make-ahead!

Chocolate Syrup, page 174	**½ cup**	**125 mL**
Chocolate Crêpes, page 169	**8**	**8**
Strawberry ice cream	**1 cup**	**250 mL**
Vanilla ice cream	**1 cup**	**250 mL**

Spread 1 tbsp. (15 mL) chocolate syrup over each crêpe.

Spoon ice cream down center making 4 strawberry and 4 vanilla. Fold crêpe over ice cream. Freeze in covered container until ready to serve. Makes 8 crêpes.

2 filled crêpes: 285 Calories; 6 g Protein; 11.3 g Total Fat; 31 g Carbohydrate; 115 mg Sodium; 2 g Dietary Fiber

Pictured below.

Velvet Chocolate Filling

So quick and simple—and smooth!

Whipping cream	**1 cup**	**250 mL**
Semisweet chocolate chips	**1⅓ cups**	**325 mL**
Brandy flavoring	**1 tsp.**	**5 mL**
Orange flavoring	**1 tsp.**	**5 mL**

Heat whipping cream in medium saucepan until boiling. Remove from heat.

Add chocolate chips. Stir until melted. Chill mixture for 1 hour.

Add brandy and orange flavorings. Beat until mixture stiffens. Makes 2⅓ cups (575 mL).

3 tbsp. (50 mL): 220 Calories; 2 g Protein; 18.9 g Total Fat; 15 g Carbohydrate; 15 mg Sodium; 2 g Dietary Fiber

Pictured below.

Chocolate Orange Filling

Use to fill Chocolate Crêpes, page 169, Chocolate Cups or Cones, page 176.

Semisweet chocolate chips	**1 cup**	**250 mL**
Skim evaporated milk	**1/3 cup**	**75 mL**
Envelope dessert topping (not prepared)	**1**	**1**
Milk	**1/3 cup**	**75 mL**
Frozen concentrated orange juice (or orange liqueur, such as Grand Marnier)	**1 tbsp.**	**15 mL**
Orange marmalade	**1 tbsp.**	**15 mL**

Heat chocolate chips and evaporated milk in small saucepan on low, stirring often, until melted and smooth. Cool to room temperature.

Beat dessert topping, milk and concentrated juice in medium bowl until stiff. Fold in marmalade. Fold in chocolate mixture until no streaks appear. Makes 3 cups (750 mL).

6 tbsp. (100 mL): 145 Calories; 2 g Protein; 8.9 g Total Fat; 17 g Carbohydrate; 27 mg Sodium; 1 g Dietary Fiber

Pictured below and page 179.

Left: Ice-Cream Crêpes, page 170
Left Center: Chocolate Crêpes, page 169,
filled with Velvet Chocolate Filling, page 170
Center Right: Chocolate Cream Crêpes, page 169
Right: Chocolate Crêpes, page 169,
filled with Chocolate Orange Filling, this page

Chocolate Cream Puffs

These can be made smaller for a dessert buffet tray. Either way, cut off tops and fill with Chocolate Orange Filling, page 171. Replace tops and drizzle with Chocolate Syrup, page 174.

Water	**1 cup**	**250 mL**
Hard margarine	**½ cup**	**125 mL**
Unsweetened chocolate baking square, cut up	**1 oz.**	**28 g**
All-purpose flour	**1 cup**	**250 mL**
Salt	**¼ tsp.**	**1 mL**
Large eggs	**4**	**4**

Heat water, margarine and chocolate in medium saucepan, stirring often, until boiling.

Add flour and salt all at once. Stir vigorously until dough cooks and leaves sides of pan forming ball (see above). Remove from heat.

Add eggs, 1 at a time, beating on medium after each addition. Spoon dough into 12 mounds on greased baking sheet, leaving room for expansion. Bake in 425°F (220°C) oven for about 25 minutes until puffs look dry. Poke sides with sharp knife to allow steam to be released. Cool on rack. Makes 12 large cream puffs or 24 smaller ones.

1 large unfilled cream puff: 150 Calories; 4 g Protein; 11.2 g Total Fat; 9 g Carbohydrate; 174 mg Sodium; 1 g Dietary Fiber

Pictured on page 173.

Black And White Eclairs

Just the treat for an afternoon tea.

Eclairs:		
Chocolate Cream Puff dough, this page		
Vanilla Filling:		
Milk	**2½ cups**	**625 mL**
Package of vanilla pudding and pie filling (not instant), 6 serving size	**1**	**1**
Cornstarch	**2 tbsp.**	**30 mL**
Milk	**½ cup**	**125 mL**
Frozen light whipped topping, thawed	**1 cup**	**250 mL**
Chocolate Glaze, page 23		

Eclairs: Spoon or pipe dough into 12 oblong shapes, 1 x 4½ inches (2.5 x 11 cm), onto greased baking sheet, leaving room for expansion. Bake in 425°F (220°C) oven for 25 minutes. Poke slit in one side of each eclair to allow steam to escape. Cool on rack.

Vanilla Filling: Heat first amount of milk in medium saucepan until just starting to boil.

Mix next 3 ingredients in small bowl. Stir into boiling milk until mixture returns to a boil and thickens. Press waxed paper over surface of pudding to prevent crust forming. Chill.

Fold topping into chilled pudding.

Cut off tops of eclairs. Fill bottoms with ¼ cup (60 mL) mixture each. Dip tops into glaze. Place on rack to set. Replace tops. Makes 12.

1 filled eclair: 352 Calories; 6 g Protein; 14.9 g Total Fat; 51 g Carbohydrate; 273 mg Sodium; 1 g Dietary Fiber

Pictured on page 173.

Top: Chocolate Cream Puffs, this page
Bottom and Center Right: Black And White Eclairs, above

Hot Chocolate Mix

A homemade necessity on your shelf. Store in airtight container.

Skim milk powder	**3 cups**	**750 mL**
Cocoa, sifted	**¾ cup**	**175 mL**
Powdered coffee whitener	**⅓ cup**	**75 mL**
Granulated sugar	**1 cup**	**250 mL**
Salt	**⅛ tsp.**	**0.5 mL**

Process all 5 ingredients in blender until well mixed. Makes 2¼ cups (560 mL).

2 tbsp. (30 mL): 134 Calories; 8 g Protein; 1.1 g Total Fat; 25 g Carbohydrate; 131 mg Sodium; 2 g Dietary Fiber

Pictured on page 175.

To Serve: 2 tbsp. (30 mL) Hot Chocolate Mix to ¾ cup (175 mL) boiling water.

Chocolate Syrup

Keep a jar in the refrigerator for a quick hot or cold drink anytime. Keeps indefinitely.

Granulated sugar	**1 cup**	**250 mL**
Cocoa, sifted	**½ cup**	**125 mL**
Cornstarch	**1 tbsp.**	**15 mL**
Salt	**⅛ tsp.**	**0.5 mL**
Hot water	**2 cups**	**500 mL**
Vanilla	**2 tsp.**	**10 mL**

Measure sugar, cocoa, cornstarch and salt into saucepan. Stir well.

Mix in hot water and vanilla. Heat until boiling, stirring constantly. Boil for 3 minutes. Makes 2½ cups (625 mL).

2 tbsp. (30 mL): 46 Calories; trace Protein; 0.2 g Total Fat; 12 g Carbohydrate; 17 mg Sodium; 1 g Dietary Fiber

Pictured on page 175.

To Serve: 2 to 3 tbsp. (30 to 50 mL) Chocolate Syrup to 1 cup (250 mL) hot or cold milk.

Instant Mocha Mix

Prepare a container of the dry ingredients to use as desired. Easy to double.

Sweetened chocolate drink powder	**1 cup**	**250 mL**
Instant coffee granules	**⅓ cup**	**75 mL**
Powdered coffee whitener	**¾ cup**	**175 mL**

Mix all 3 ingredients together. Store in airtight container in cupboard. Makes about 2 cups (500 mL), enough for 16 servings.

2 tbsp. (30 mL): 72 Calories; 1 g Protein; 2.2 g Total Fat; 13 g Carbohydrate; 33 mg Sodium; 0 g Dietary Fiber

Pictured on page 175.

Instant Mocha

Stir 2 tbsp. (30 mL) Instant Mocha Mix into 1 cup (250 mL) boiling water. Stir well. Top with 2 tbsp. (30 mL) whipped topping. Serves 1.

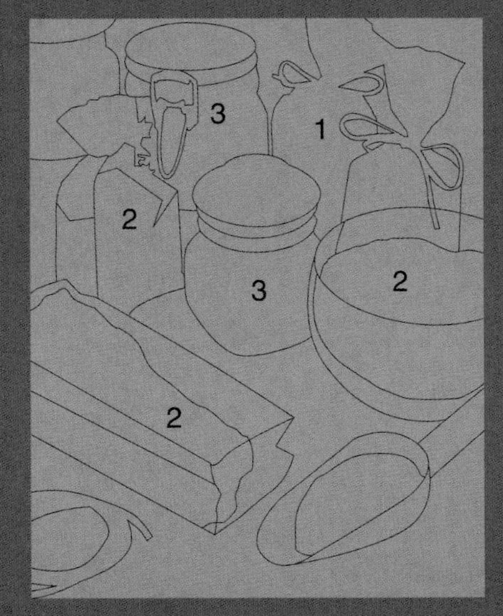

1. Instant Mocha Mix, above
2. Hot Chocolate Mix, this page
3. Chocolate Syrup, this page

Chocolate Cups

Keep melted chocolate in bowl in warm water in container for easy handling.

Dark chocolate dipping wafers, melted (or semisweet chocolate baking squares, tempered, page 12, and remelted)	**6 oz.**	**170 g**

TULIP CUP

Spoon generous amount of chocolate on flat working surface, such as marble slab. Dip bottom end of small, clean, expanded balloon into chocolate. Maintaining contact with chocolate, angle balloon each of four directions, creating 4 "petals." Leaving balloon in, chill overnight until dry and firm. Snip tiny hole near knot at top of balloon to allow air to escape slowly. Carefully remove balloon.

Pictured on page 178 and page 179.

CRINKLE CUP (FOIL)

Press foil firmly inside bottom and sides of custard cup. Apply chocolate to bottom and sides using paintbrush or small pastry brush. Chill for 10 minutes. Use remaining chocolate to fill in thin areas. Chill overnight until dry and firm. Gently lift foil out of cup. Carefully peel foil from chocolate. Foil cups may also be used.

CRINKLE CUP (PLASTIC WRAP)

Press plastic wrap firmly inside bottom and sides of dampened custard cup. Use small spoon to drizzle chocolate down insides of cup until fully coated. Cover bottom. Chill for 10 minutes. Use remaining chocolate to fill in thin areas. Chill overnight until dry and firm. Gently lift out of cup. Carefully peel plastic from chocolate.

Chocolate Cones

Fill these with Chocolate Whipped Topping, page 109, or Chantilly Butter Crunch, page 178.

Dark chocolate dipping wafers, melted (or semisweet chocolate baking squares, tempered, page 12, and remelted)	**4 oz.**	**113 g**

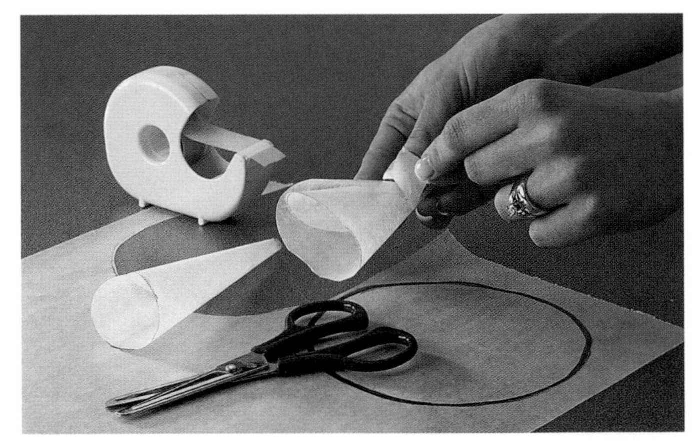

Cut eight 4 inch (10 cm) circles from regular weight or construction paper. Form into cones of equal size. Tape to hold shape. Place in homemade stand.

Cut eight 5 inch (12.5 cm) circles from parchment paper. Form into cones of equal size, making sure bottom point is tightly closed. Insert into paper cones.

Place piece of cardboard over dish or turn shallow box upside down. Cut eight 1/2 inch (12 mm) holes a few inches apart to create stand for construction paper cones.

Pour 2 tsp. (10 mL) melted chocolate into parchment paper cone. Using paintbrush, bring chocolate up from bottom, all around inside of cone to top edge. Coat evenly. Stand cone in box. Repeat with remaining cones. Chill.

Gently lift parchment cone from paper cone. Carefully peel parchment away from chocolate cone. Chill. Makes 8 cones.

1 unfilled cone: 67 Calories; 1 g Protein; 5.6 g Total Fat; 7 g Carbohydrate; trace Sodium; 0 g Dietary Fiber

Pictured on page 178 and page 179.

Chocolate Mousse

Soft and creamy. Pure bliss. Do not freeze.

Semisweet chocolate chips	**1 cup**	**250 mL**
Egg yolks (large)	**4**	**4**
Vanilla	**1/2 tsp.**	**2 mL**
Egg whites (large), room temperature	**4**	**4**
Icing (confectioner's) sugar	**1/4 cup**	**60 mL**
Whipping cream (or 2 cups, 500 mL, whipped topping)	**1 cup**	**250 mL**

Melt chocolate chips in medium saucepan over hot water, or on low, stirring constantly, until smooth. Do not overheat. Remove from heat.

Add egg yolks and vanilla. Beat well. Transfer to large bowl.

Using clean beaters, beat egg whites in separate bowl until soft peaks form. Add icing sugar gradually, continuing to beat until stiff.

Using same beaters, beat whipping cream in small bowl until stiff. Gently fold whites into chocolate mixture. Fold in whipped cream. Turn into individual serving dishes. Chill. Makes generous 4 3/4 cups (1.2 L), enough for 6 servings.

1 serving: 323 Calories; 6 g Protein; 25.6 g Total Fat; 21 g Carbohydrate; 61 mg Sodium; 2 g Dietary Fiber

Pictured on page 179.

Chocolate Mocha Mousse

Such a light color because of added whipped topping. Has a good texture. Serve with a bit of whipped topping and grated chocolate.

Semisweet chocolate chips	**1 1/2 cups**	**375 mL**
Butter (or hard margarine)	**2 tbsp.**	**30 mL**
Hot coffee	**1/3 cup**	**75 mL**
Egg yolks (large)	**4**	**4**
Granulated sugar	**1/3 cup**	**75 mL**
Egg whites (large), room temperature	**4**	**4**
Frozen light whipped topping, thawed	**2 cups**	**500 mL**

Put first 3 ingredients into large saucepan. Heat on low, stirring constantly, until smooth.

Beat in egg yolks, 2 at a time. Beat in sugar. Remove from heat. Cool to room temperature.

Using clean beaters, beat egg whites in medium bowl until stiff. Gently fold into chocolate mixture. Fold in whipped topping. Turn into individual serving dishes. Chill. Do not freeze. Makes generous 5 cups (1.25 L), enough for 6 servings.

1 serving: 379 Calories; 6 g Protein; 23.9 g Total Fat; 41 g Carbohydrate; 94 mg Sodium; 2 g Dietary Fiber

Pictured on page 178 and 179.

Chantilly Butter Crunch

So tasty in Chocolate Cups, page 176.

Butter (or hard margarine)	**½ cup**	**125 mL**
Brown sugar, packed	**¼ cup**	**60 mL**
All-purpose flour	**1 cup**	**250 mL**
Finely chopped pecans	**½ cup**	**125 mL**
Whipping cream (or 2 cups, 500 mL, whipped topping)	**1 cup**	**250 mL**
Granulated sugar	**1 tbsp.**	**15 mL**
Vanilla	**1 tsp.**	**5 mL**

Melt butter in medium saucepan. Stir in brown sugar, flour and pecans. Press in ungreased 9 x 9 inch (22 x 22 cm) pan. Bake in 375°F (190°C) oven for about 15 minutes until nicely browned. Stir with spoon to crumble. Cool.

Beat whipping cream, granulated sugar and vanilla in small bowl until stiff. Fold in crumb mixture. Makes 4 cups (1 L).

⅓ cup (75 mL): 232 Calories; 2 g Protein; 18.4 g Total Fat; 16 g Carbohydrate; 92 mg Sodium; 1 g Dietary Fiber

Pictured on page 178 and page 179.

Chocolate Cups, page 176, and Chocolate Cones, page 176, filled with:
1. Cassata Filling, page 113
2. Chocolate Mousse, page 177
3. White Chocolate Mousse, page 180
4. Chantilly Butter Crunch, above
5. Chocolate Orange Filling, page 171
6. Chocolate Mocha Mousse, page 177

White Chocolate Mousse

A rich, soft mousse. Best eaten fresh.

Granulated sugar	2/3 cup	150 mL
Water	1/4 cup	60 mL
White chocolate chips	1 cup	250 mL
Whipping cream (or 2 cups, 500 mL, whipped topping)	1 cup	250 mL
Vanilla	1 tsp.	5 mL

Stir sugar and water in saucepan on medium heat until sugar is dissolved.

Add chocolate chips. Stir until melted and smooth. Cool saucepan in cold water in sink. Chill. Whisk until smooth.

Beat whipping cream and vanilla in small bowl until stiff. Fold into chocolate mixture. Turn into individual serving dishes. Makes 3 cups (750 mL).

1/2 cup (125 mL): 361 Calories; 3 g Protein; 21.4 g Total Fat; 40g Carbohydrate; 37 mg Sodium; 0 g Dietary Fiber

Pictured on page 178 and 179.

Chocolate And Cherry Terrine

Allow extra time to make this incredible dessert. It's worth every minute.

Cake:

Egg yolks (large)	6	6
Granulated sugar	3/4 cup	175 mL
Butter (not margarine), melted	1/3 cup	75 mL
All-purpose flour	1/2 cup	125 mL
Cocoa, sifted	1/3 cup	75 mL
Egg whites (large), room temperature	6	6

White Chocolate Cherry Mousse:

Envelope of unflavored gelatin	1/4 oz.	7 g
Water	1/4 cup	60 mL
Mini white chocolate chips	1 1/2 cups	375 mL
Kirsch liqueur	3 tbsp.	50 mL
Egg whites (large), room temperature	3	3
Whipping cream	1 cup	250 mL
Egg yolks (large)	3	3
Maraschino cherries, finely chopped, patted dry with paper towel	8	8
Chocolate Glaze, page 23		
Mini white chocolate chips	1/4 cup	60 mL

Cake: Grease 10 x 15 inch (25 x 38 cm) jelly roll pan. Line bottom with greased waxed paper. Beat egg yolks in medium bowl for about 3 minutes, gradually adding sugar until light in color, increased in volume and thickened. Beat in melted butter slowly until blended. Gradually add flour and cocoa while beating on low.

Using clean beaters, beat egg whites in large bowl until stiff but not dry. Do not overbeat. Gradually fold egg white mixture into batter until no streaks remain. Turn into prepared pan. Bake in 350°F (175°C) oven for about 20 minutes. Turn out onto tea towel that has been dusted with icing (confectioner's) sugar. Peel off waxed paper. Cool.

Carefully cut rectangular pieces from cooled cake to fit bottom, sides and top of 9 x 5 x 3 inch (22 x 12.5 x 7.5 cm) loaf pan that has been lined with overhanging plastic wrap.

White Chocolate Cherry Mousse: Sprinkle gelatin over water in small saucepan. Let stand for 1 minute. Heat and stir until gelatin is dissolved. Reduce heat to low.

Stir in chocolate chips until melted. Remove from heat. Add liqueur. Stir. Cool to room temperature.

Beat egg whites in medium bowl until stiff but not dry. Set aside.

Beat whipping cream in small bowl until stiff.

Beat egg yolks in large bowl for about 5 minutes until thick and light in color. Add chocolate mixture. Beat for 3 minutes. Fold in egg whites. Fold in whipped cream.

Add cherries. Fold in. Spoon into cake-lined pan, not quite to top of cake.

Cover with cake piece for top. Cover with plastic wrap. Chill overnight.

Turn out loaf from pan. Carefully remove plastic wrap. Turn loaf, upside down, on wire rack set on waxed paper.

Pour glaze over top and down sides, using a knife if desired to smooth. Top and sides should be coated with thin covering of chocolate.

Place white chocolate chips in small freezer bag. Heat in microwave on low for 10 second intervals until melted. May also be melted by setting bag in hot water. Snip small hole in corner of bag. Squeeze chocolate through hole in thin design over top and sides of loaf. Store in refrigerator. Do not freeze. Cuts into 10 slices.

1 slice: 559 Calories; 10 g Protein; 36.6 g Total Fat; 47 g Carbohydrate; 207 mg Sodium; 2 g Dietary Fiber

Pictured on page 182/183.

Measurement Tables

Throughout this book measurements are given in Conventional and Metric measure. To compensate for differences between the two measurements due to rounding, a full metric measure is not always used. The cup used is the standard 8 fluid ounce. Temperature is given in degrees Fahrenheit and Celsius. Baking pan measurements are in inches and centimetres as well as quarts and litres. An exact metric conversion is given on this page as well as the working equivalent (Standard Measure).

Oven Temperatures

Fahrenheit (°F)	Celsius (°C)	Fahrenheit (°F)	Celsius (°C)
175°	80°	350°	175°
200°	95°	375°	190°
225°	110°	400°	205°
250°	120°	425°	220°
275°	140°	450°	230°
300°	150°	475°	240°
325°	160°	500°	260°

Spoons

Conventional Measure	Metric Exact Conversion Millilitre (mL)	Metric Standard Measure Millilitre (mL)
1/8 teaspoon (tsp.)	0.6 mL	0.5 mL
1/4 teaspoon (tsp.)	1.2 mL	1 mL
1/2 teaspoon (tsp.)	2.4 mL	2 mL
1 teaspoon (tsp.)	4.7 mL	5 mL
2 teaspoons (tsp.)	9.4 mL	10 mL
1 tablespoon (tbsp.)	14.2 mL	15 mL

Cups

1/4 cup (4 tbsp.)	56.8 mL	60 mL
1/3 cup (5 1/3 tbsp.)	75.6 mL	75 mL
1/2 cup (8 tbsp.)	113.7 mL	125 mL
2/3 cup (10 2/3 tbsp.)	151.2 mL	150 mL
3/4 cup (12 tbsp.)	170.5 mL	175 mL
1 cup (16 tbsp.)	227.3 mL	250 mL
4 1/2 cups	1022.9 mL	1000 mL (1 L)

Pans

Conventional Inches	Metric Centimetres
8x8 inch	20x20 cm
9x9 inch	22x22 cm
9x13 inch	22x33 cm
10x15 inch	25x38 cm
11x17 inch	28x43 cm
8x2 inch round	20x5 cm
9x2 inch round	22x5 cm
10x4 1/2 inch tube	25x11 cm
8x4x3 inch loaf	20x10x7.5 cm
9x5x3 inch loaf	22x12.5x7.5 cm

Dry Measurements

Conventional Measure Ounces (oz.)	Metric Exact Conversion Grams (g)	Metric Standard Measure Grams (g)
1 oz.	28.3 g	28 g
2 oz.	56.7 g	57 g
3 oz.	85.0 g	85 g
4 oz.	113.4 g	125 g
5 oz.	141.7 g	140 g
6 oz.	170.1 g	170 g
7 oz.	198.4 g	200 g
8 oz.	226.8 g	250 g
16 oz.	453.6 g	500 g
32 oz.	907.2 g	1000 g (1 kg)

Casseroles

Canada & Britain		United States	
Standard Size Casserole	Exact Metric Measure	Standard Size Casserole	Exact Metric Measure
1 qt. (5 cups)	1.13 L	1 qt. (4 cups)	900 mL
1 1/2 qts. (7 1/2 cups)	1.69 L	1 1/2 qts. (6 cups)	1.35 L
2 qts. (10 cups)	2.25 L	2 qts. (8 cups)	1.8 L
2 1/2 qts. (12 1/2 cups)	2.81 L	2 1/2 qts. (10 cups)	2.25 L
3 qts. (15 cups)	3.38 L	3 qts. (12 cups)	2.7 L
4 qts. (20 cups)	4.5 L	4 qts. (16 cups)	3.6 L
5 qts. (25 cups)	5.63 L	5 qts. (20 cups)	4.5 L

D

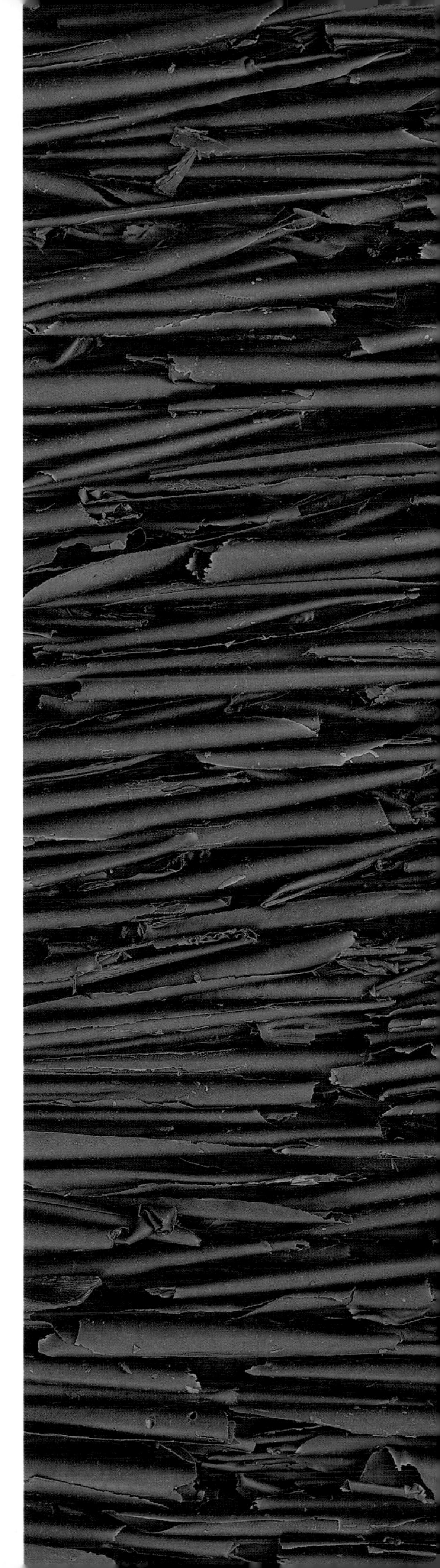